ANTHOLOGY OF LOVE AND DEATH VOL. 2

Anthology of Love and Death Vol. 2

MARIE JOSEPH-CHARLES

Contents

Dedication		viii
1	The Way They Used to be	1
2	Remember	34
3	Seek truth	35
4	Addiction	36
5	Written in my Sleep at 430am	43
6	Soulmates	45
7	Overwhelmed	46
8	A Little Love Poem	48
9	The Truth Shall Set You Free	49
10	Grace	65
11	Eclipse 2024 Poem A	66
12	Jailbird	67
13	The Flight Home	69
14	No One	70
15	When You Want It Done	71
16	Death of innocence	72
17	Listen up, Men	74
18	The Fight	75
19	Questioning Love	77

20	My Knight Var. 2	78
21	The Light	81
22	December 3rd	91
23	Alive	92
24	Belgium and Blood	94
25	August 9th	101
26	August 19th Poem A	102
27	Lies you sing	104
28	September 1st	106
29	The Pain no one Talks About	108
30	The Road of Marriage	111
31	The Art Museum	112
32	The Tracks	113
33	Giver and Taker	115
34	Broken Trust	117
35	To Blame	119
36	Sticks and Stones	121
37	The Joy of Halloween	123
38	Iliana the Monster	125
39	Respiratory Infection	156
40	Onward	157
41	A Christmas Poem	159
42	New Year 2024/2025	160

Notes   161

Copyright © 2025 by Madison Schleibaum
All rights reserved. No part of this book may be reproduced in any manner whatsoever without written permission except in the case of brief quotations embodied in critical articles and reviews.
First Printing, 2025

In dedication to the wonderful people who have supported me and enjoy my novels, short stories, and poetry.

Chapter 1

The Way They Used to be

How did this ever work? I stare at my hands in my lap. They look dark against my pale legs. On this hot summer day, I had caved and wore shorts to the lake. My legs dangle over the edge of the dock made of plywood screwed to blue plastic barrels. I can barely see my toes in the water that is both murky and sparkling as the ripples almost twinkle in the afternoon sun. I'm trying so hard to stop the tears that are making the ripples but I can't hold them back. My body aches from sobbing. My chest feels concave, collapsed in on a heart that is no longer whole. We were Romeo and Juliet, only they had a happier ending.

Steven Michael Sherman III, Trey, as I know him, was the boy in the big white house. It is a mansion. It is tall and wide with pillars holding up the front of the black roof that matches the black decorative shutters. The guest drive creates a U-shape in front of the house around a carefully cultivated flowerbed at its center. The family drive continues on to the back of the house to the expansive garage that houses Steven Michael Sherman II's most prized possession, his car collection.

Trey hardly sees his parents. In a six-bedroom, six-bathroom home that can touch the clouds, it is easy to go a day or two without seeing each other. That is if his parents are even home.

His dad is often jet-setting to exotic locations. His wife, Autumn Sherman, joins him for shopping, to act as eye candy, and to glean gossip from the other wives. Her job in the family business is to be perfect, gain the trust of both partners and competitors, and feed information to her husband. Trey is often left alone to while away pointless hours in front of the television screen during the summers he would come home from the private school he attended.

I remember being a little girl and looking at the big white house at the other end of the lake when we drove by. I wondered what kind of people lived there and how many servants they had. I wondered if I would ever live in a house so big or imagined what it was like to live in such a place.

I live on the other end of the lake and my family's estate is not quite so grand. Our landscaping is less tulips and roses and more tomatoes and cucumbers. Where the Shermans have been known to rent swans to waddle around their parties, we have a steady stock of chickens including one ill-tempered rooster known as Cockzilla who once took on a hawk that attacked our hens... and the rooster won. The Shermans have a heated cement drive; we have ruts in cracked old blacktop. The Shermans have six bedrooms (not including where the maid lives) while we have three. The Shermans have a finished basement. Our house sits on cinderblocks inhabited by a couple hundred spiders and one opossum that seems to have struck a truce with Cockzilla. Mr. Sherman is always tidy and appears ready for any occasion. Daddy has a dark cast to his skin from all the coal dust from the mines and his fingernails are never clean.

But Daddy loves me. He says I am the diamond that comes from all that coal. It's just been the two of us in that house since Momma died in a car accident when I was nine. She left Daddy to support us and I had to grow up a little faster than planned. I stepped up, tending to the garden and the chickens and keeping the house clean. I didn't get to play with the other kids outside of school much on account of so many responsibilities. At first, I didn't mind. Whenever Daddy and I went to the store and I carried one of Momma's old pocketbooks, I felt too grown up for such childish things as friends. After a while, though, it started to ache. It was a lot of work to keep up with grades and the house. I wanted to join a team or choir or... something. Kelly is probably the closest thing I have to a best friend. After Momma died, we didn't get to play so much after school or on weekends, but we were there for every birthday party the other one had. She lived up the road a-ways and would sometimes come down to spend time with me while I did chores or to do homework together.

For years my life was simple, quiet, a bit dull, but mostly happy. Then I turned fifteen and that summer changed everything.

I was floating in the lake in a bathing suit and shorts – the same ones I'm wearing now, actually. I was just drifting and letting the world vanish. The chickens were fed. The wash was done. Daddy wouldn't be home for hours. I didn't have a care in the world and let myself move as if I was a part of the lake.

Suddenly, I was lifted out of the water. I screamed and punched just like I'd been taught to. I felt my fist make contact with something before I was dropped back into the water. I came back up sputtering, flailing, and ready to fight.

"Easy! Easy! Would you calm down?" my attacker said.

I pushed my wet hair out of my eyes and held up my fists. I had to blink a few times to get the water out of my eyes and make sure I saw him clearly because I didn't believe it. He was beautiful. He looked a year or so older than me. He was blonde, not a brown-blonde like me, but a golden blonde you see in movie stars. His eyes were so blue they looked like pieces of the sky. He was rubbing a reddening part of his jaw.

"You alright?" he asked.

I found my voice and suddenly felt anger toward the handsome stranger who had attempted to abduct me. "What the HELL did you think you're doing?" I screamed.

We were standing in water just over our knees near a steep bank. I looked around quickly and carefully, not wanting to take my eyes off of him in case he tried something again. I didn't recognize where I was and felt myself begin to panic.

"I saw a body floating in the lake. I thought you might need help."

"So? So, what? You'd thought you'd be a hero?" I let my arms fall to my sides.

"I just wanted to help," he said again.

"Well, apart from the heart attack you just gave me, I'm fine," I snapped and turned toward the bank.

"No, you're not. You're bleeding."

I turned back and he was pointing at my leg. Sure enough, the back of my calf was bleeding from a pretty serious cut. I must have sliced it on a rock when he dropped me. The gash was about three inches long and leaving a trail of red down my leg and into the calm water.

"Let me take you back to my house and have Martha clean that up for you," he offered.

"I'm not going to a stranger's house," I said belligerently and turned back to the edge of the lake.

It was steep here and I struggled to pull myself out. The wall of the lake was about shoulder level and my feet kept slipping, refusing to find a secure foothold.

He stood behind me. "Do you want some help?"

"No," I said defiantly.

"Okay then."

I continued to struggle and continued to slip. Breathing out heavily, fully exasperated, I backed up and assessed my situation. I realized he was now standing at the top of the bank and looking down at me.

"Are you sure you don't want some help?" he asked.

I scowled at him. He chuckled and pointed to his left. I looked over and saw tree roots protruding from the clay and the side of the mud wall.

"Makes a good ladder," he stated plainly.

I looked around in an attempt to find another way. I did *not* want him to have the satisfaction of knowing I had to listen to him. Unfortunately, there was no other way in sight. With a huff, I marched over to the tree roots and grabbed a hold. I hoisted myself up and over onto the ledge and back on solid ground. I sat for a moment and assessed my leg. The wound was fairly deep and still bleeding.

"Please let me help you with that," he said. His voice was earnest and the look on his face expressed genuine concern.

I looked at him for a long minute. "How far is it?" I asked.

He pointed and I looked over. He was pointing at the big white house that I had dreamed about on the North shore of the lake. We were only a few minute's walk away. I looked back at my leg. Grudgingly, I agreed to go with him. Daddy would have never approved but he seemed a little young to be a serial killer. I raised myself to my feet and limped along behind him.

"My name is Trey by the way," he said. "And you are?"

"Sarah," I said flatly.

"I'm really sorry I scared you, Sarah. I really did think you were in distress."

"And you just wanted to play hero?" I shot at him again.

"No, I just didn't want a rotted corpse stinking up my lake," he shot back.

We continued to walk in silence. We walked up the U-bend of the driveway. The house was even bigger than I had dreamed. There was so much detail in the pillars and the stones in the garden than I had ever discerned from the road. I actually felt the shadow of it pass over me like a cloud of doom. We continue straight past the front door. He stopped.

"Oh. We should go in the front," he said.

"Does it matter?" I asked.

"Of course it matters," he said indignantly. "The front door is for guests and you are my guest."

I felt a little more like a hostage than a guest but I couldn't stop myself from smiling weekly at him. I tripped trying to get up the steps and felt a shooting pain in my leg. He helped me up and supported me to the front door. His hand was warm even compared to the heat of the day. He held the front door open for me and led me inside.

We could fit my entire house in that foyer. The floor was white marble and the walls were pristine white too. I had felt a sense of meekness when we had passed the columns guarding the front door but that feeling was nothing compared to how insignificant I felt inside. The ceiling was high and vaulted. There was a gilded mirror surrounded by potted plants immediately to the right. I saw halls and doorways leading off into oblivion. I could imagine getting lost for weeks in a house that size.

We heard a shriek and looked over. A woman in black slacks and a white blouse wearing an apron was staring with her mouth agape. "Mr. Trey! What is the meaning of this?"

"Martha! My friend Sarah here requires your assistance."

"Your friend Sarah is bleeding all over the entryway floor!"

I looked down and there was indeed a significant puddle of blood surrounding my bare foot. I felt my face flush with embarrassment.

"And that is exactly why I brought her to you. She requires your expert medical care." He smiled at the housekeeper.

"Mr. Trey I am CPR certified. I am not a triage nurse," she said flatly but she rolled her eyes and stomped off returning only moments later with a first aid kit and a bucket of warm soapy water.

She placed the bucket at my feet. "Please, Sarah," she said. "Wash your leg in this."

"*Miss* Sarah," Trey emphasized. "She is a guest just like any that my parents bring into this house."

A flash of annoyance crossed Martha's face.

"It's okay," I said quietly.

"No, it's not," Trey stated. "You deserve every bit of respect that anyone else who enters this house gets."

I felt my face warm once again.

Martha slid the bucket an inch closer to my leg. "*Miss* Sarah," she said. "If you please."

I nodded and stuck my foot in the bucket. I took the proffered rag from her hand and washed the wound carefully. I could only imagine what had gotten into it from the murky lake water. When the wound looked sufficiently flushed, I pulled my leg out of the bucket and took a towel that Martha handed me. I patted and dried my leg gingerly, but the wound continued to bleed. Martha then took a fistful of gauze from the first aid kit and pressed it against the gash firmly.

"Hold this here and apply pressure, if you please." The irritation in her voice was getting stronger.

I bent down and twisted awkwardly to apply the gauze to the back of my calf.

"Let me help," Trey said and he dropped to his knee pressing his left hand firmly against the gauze and the other against my shin.

"Mr. Trey!" Martha exclaimed. "There is no reason for you to expose yourself to this biohazard."

"Martha!" Trey looked sternly at her. "She is a girl, not a toxic waste barrel."

Martha pursed her lips and began fussing with other items in the first aid kit while Trey looked at me apologetically. Martha removed the gauze from my leg and the bleeding had slowed significantly. She then took elastic bandages and stretched them across the wound like stitches to hold it closed. She put more gauze over the bandages and wrapped my leg in medical tape.

"Miss Sarah should probably see a doctor as soon as possible," she said flatly as she mopped up the blood on the floor with the towel and took the bucket, towel, and first aid kit and marched into the other room.

"I'm sorry about her," Trey said. "She can be a little snobbish sometimes."

"It really is okay," I said.

"Come on," he said. "Let's get something cold to drink and I will take you home."

He smiled as he led me through the entryway and down a hall. We then went down a flight of stairs and into a basement kitchen. I had never seen so many gadgets in my entire life. We had an oven, a toaster, a microwave, and a coffee maker. I saw multiple ovens and stove tops, an espresso machine, a blender that looked like it could pulverize stone, and other assorted things that I didn't even recognize. I knew my eyes were bulging when he smiled at me.

"My parents entertain a lot," he said. "As my dad says, 'with certain status comes certain obligations,'" he made a mocking voice. "We have everything we need to make big meals for their guests. Mom always says, there's money to be made in good impressions."

He led me over to a granite island and pulled out a stool for me to sit on. Despite my guide, I felt like a trespasser in a foreign land.

He held out a bottle of water and a soda pop. "Which would you like?"

I tapped the pop and he set it in front of me. He walked back to the refrigerator and returned with one of his own. He cracked it open and I opened mine. He tapped his to mine gently as if a toast and took a long deep drink followed by a slight belch.

"I'm not allowed to drink from the can when my parents are home," he admitted.

I cocked my head at him. "What do you drink from?"

He laughed. "Glasses, of course."

I grit my teeth at my stupidity.

"Do you live around the lake?" he asked.

I nodded. "On the South shore," I said.

"How long have you lived there?"

I shrugged. "My whole life."

"Really? How come I've never seen you before?"

"I don't normally swim this far from home."

"Do you swim in that water often?"

"Every summer. Every chance I get."

"Really? My parents would never let me actually go *in* the lake. Honestly, if they found out I jumped in to save you today they would probably yell at me."

"Are they afraid you'll drown?"

He laughed. "No. They say it's unsanitary."

"They probably aren't wrong but it ain't killed me yet," I said.

He laughed. "Is it deep?"

I shook my head. "Not in the summer. That's why the banks are so steep right now. In the spring when the snow melts and comes down off the mountain and the rainy season hits, it's pretty deep."

He nodded. "I'm not usually home in the spring. I live at my school most of the year."

"You live at school?"

"Yeah. My parents believe it'll help me make the 'right sort of friends.'" He made finger quotes around the last part of the sentence. "Where do you go to school?" he asked.

I felt a little sheepish. "I just go to the county high school like everybody else around here." I looked at him. "Almost everybody else."

He grinned wide. "What's it like?"

I shrugged. "It's school. We march from one class to the next and take tests and such."

"Do you have clubs and friends and stuff?"

"I don't have too many friends. A couple of good ones though, I guess. I don't belong to any of the clubs or anything. I don't really have time for them."

"Why not?"

"I have a lot of chores and stuff at home," I said quietly.

He nodded. "You're lucky. I have to spend an hour a day practicing the violin and another hour every day practicing the piano. Then there's the debate club and the math club and lacrosse."

"You sound like you're really busy," I said.

He nodded. "That doesn't mean I want to be though," he said dolefully. "Busy doesn't mean happy, you know?"

We finished our sodas and went back up the stairs towards the main body of the house.

"Let me take you home," he said.

I did not want this boy who was so very handsome and had been so kind to me to see my tiny little house. I had never been embarrassed by my home before this and I felt ashamed of my embarrassment.

"That's okay," I said. "I can walk."

"Don't start getting stubborn again," he said. "Your leg could break open from moving around too much. They'll find you bled out on the side of the road. I promise I haven't kidnapped you yet and I have no intention of doing it now."

I felt myself smile again. "Okay."

He led me out a double glass French door and into another driveway towards the garage. He pulled out his keys and clicked a button. The garage door on the far right opened revealing a shiny, black Lexus.

"Is that your car?" I breathed.

He nodded. "It's my mom's old car; it's not new or anything."

I raised my eyebrows. There was not a scratch on it, the paint gleamed in the sunlight. No cracks in the windshield and the mirrors actually belonged to the car. What did he mean it was old? We walked into the garage and he opened the passenger side door for me. I slid into the warm leather seat and pulled in my legs. He closed the door behind me. He got in on his side and pressed the ignition. It didn't even need a key! I barely felt the car rumble to life, not like Daddy's truck that vibrated your teeth. He pulled out of the driveway and then up their private road and stopped.

"Left or right?"

I thought for a moment. I had never been on this end of the lake and needed a moment to get my bearings. "Left, I think."

He nodded, turned on the blinker, looked both ways, and pulled out. As we got closer to home, I felt my nerves worsening. I didn't see any reason he would ever want to speak to me or see me again but yet I feared that if he saw where I lived, he would certainly never return.

"It's that one," I said quietly as I pointed to the left.

My driveway was long and paved but not smooth like the Sherman's. We didn't even have a garage. But the siding was intact and the roof was sturdy.

"Are those chickens?" he asked excitedly.

"Yes?"

"I've never seen a chicken that wasn't on a plate! Can I touch one?"

I stared at him and tried to decide if he was pulling my leg or not but his eyes were locked on the birds scattered around the front yard.

"I guess so," I said.

"Awesome!"

He parked the car at the top of the drive in front of the house. He opened his door but immediately yelped and slammed it shut again. I looked just in time to see a flurry of reddish-brown feathers hit his window. Cockzilla was defending his flock.

"Oh. Sorry about that. Our rooster is a little territorial. Let me put him up and then you can get out."

I got out of the car and walked around to the other side of it. I felt Trey's eyes on me as I stalked up to the two-foot-tall bird whose feathers were puffed out at me. I dove and grabbed him as he made another leap at the car. I heard applause from inside the car and felt laughter bubbling up out of my chest as I walked the angry bird back to his pen around the coop. When he was secured inside, I motioned for Trey to get out of the car.

"How many chickens do you have?" he asked. "And are they all that mean?"

"No. Just the rooster. We have about twenty or so of them."

"Do you eat their eggs?"

"Yes. They're good for breakfast and baking cookies and that," I said.

"That's so cool! Which one can I touch?"

I felt a little mean streak burn inside me. "Hold on a minute," I said. I walked over to the feed bin and took out a scoop. I handed it to him. "Shake this," I said.

He looked at me cautiously but did as he was told. Twenty hens came running from all corners of the property directly at him. He yelled and I laughed. They all flocked around him and stood expectantly, waiting to be fed.

"Scatter it around the ground," I instructed.

He did so and the birds pecked happily. I could hear Cockzilla fussing behind me at not being part of the feeding.

"You can touch any of them now," I said. "They're distracted."

He had a wildly excited look in his eye as he crouched down and put his hand on the bird closest to him.

"They're so soft!" he exclaimed. "That's not what I was expecting at all."

I watched him carefully touch each bird in turn. I couldn't imagine being so excited or fascinated by chickens.

"Are they hard to take care of?" he asked.

"No."

"What did I just feed them?"

"Chicken feed."

"I'm not allowed to have any pets. I'm only home in the summer and my dad doesn't really like animals. My mom used to have a little dog with buggy eyes that she carried in her purse but it was hard to get in and out of the country when they travel and Martha complained if they left it behind."

"That's sad. I couldn't imagine not having Tom around."

"Which one's Tom? That big angry one?"

I laughed. "No. He's a pet, not a chicken."

I clicked my tongue a few times and up from a sunny spot on our homemade dock, right where I had left him, rose a fat, orange ball of fur. It stretched leisurely and walked toward us.

"A cat!" Trey turned his outstretched hand toward Tom who gladly rubbed his face on it.

"We have a few cats around here that I feed but Tom's the only one that's really a pet."

"That's so cool!"

"I want a dog but Daddy says when I go off to college in a few years he won't have time to take care of it."

"What about your mom?" Trey asked, still delighted with the cat that had now rolled on his back and allowed his belly to be rubbed.

"She died a while back. It's just me and Daddy."

He looked up at me soberly. "I-I'm sorry."

"It's okay," I assured him.

"No brothers or sisters?"

I shook my head. "You?"

"I kind of have an older sister. Her mom was my dad's first wife. They don't talk to us because they call my mom a home-wrecker."

"That's mean."

He shrugged his shoulder. "Truth isn't always nice. Dad filed for divorce because my mom is younger and prettier."

We were quiet a little longer. He allowed himself to be reabsorbed by the fat ginger cat and the chickens, having confirmed there was not a morsel of feed left, dispersed. Finally, he stood and brushed his hands on his shorts, still damp from his heroics in the lake.

"How's your leg?"

"Doesn't hurt at all," I lied.

He grinned. "Well, Martha will want me home for supper soon."

I nodded and held my hand out for him to shake. "Thank you for having her patch of my leg and bringing me home."

He looked stunned for a second. He took my hand in his but did not shake it. "My pleasure, Sarah. I'm glad we met." He rubbed his jaw with his free hand. "And thanks for giving me something to remember you by."

I was blushing. I knew I was blushing and I couldn't keep a silly grin from creeping across my face. "Me too. And let that be a lesson about damsels in distress."

I watched him get back into his fancy car, now soiled with dust, and back out onto the road. I saw his arm over the roof of his car as he gave a final wave before speeding off. I felt a nudge at my feet. I looked down and Tom's big, yellow eyes gazed up into mine.

"Well, I hope you didn't like him too much." I picked up my cat and kissed the top of his soft head. "We're probably never going to see him again."

That night at supper, I told Daddy all about my would-be hero who ended up injuring me instead.

"Well, I thank him for lookin' out for ya," he said through a mouthful of mashed potatoes. "But you really ought to be more careful."

"Daddy, do you know anyone who knows these woods better than me?"

He swallowed. "No. But just because you know every boulder and bush doesn't mean you know the people."

I conceded his point and promised to be more careful.

The next day was a true summer storm. The day was almost as dark as nighttime except when there was a lightning strike. In the distance, I could hear a tree get struck and the sound shook the house. Tom stayed snuggled against my hip for most of the day while I lounged on the couch reading my library book. I periodically caught myself thinking about what was going on in the big white house. I bet they couldn't even hear the raindrops on the roof.

The morning after the storm, I stood on the front porch and looked around. The damage was bad but not severe. A good-sized branch had come down off the oak tree and hit the chicken coop but the roof remained intact. There were smaller bits and twigs on the ground and the lake had risen a few inches. I decided to just mow over the little things and pick up the bigger stuff as I went. But first, I needed to get the branch off the coop. The leafy part was stuck on the roof and the rest of the branch trailed down to the ground. It was too big to move by myself so I went to the shed and retrieved the saw. As I began to cut, I heard tires on the drive and looked up. There was the black Lexus, spattered with fresh mud.

"Hi!" he called as he got out, eyes darting left and right in case he was spotted by the attack rooster.

"Hi yourself," I said. "He's locked up, by the way. What are you doing here?"

I could hear the genuine surprise in my voice and hoped he couldn't. Judging by his perfect smile, he had.

"Came to see if you got washed away with that storm."

"I ain't."

"What are you doing?" He examined the saw in my hand.

"I've got to cut up this branch so I can move it."

He walked from one side of the branch to the other, studying it. "How can I help?"

I was a little taken aback by the offer. "Uh. I guess just keep it from moving on me."

"Done." He propped his shoulder under it as high up as it would go and braced it in place with his hands.

We made short work of the branch. We eventually cut it into four pieces and hauled them off to be used in a bonfire.

"What's next?" he asked.

"I've got to get the other big branches cleared out of the yard and mow over everything else." I indicated the push mower in the shed with the doors still stood open.

"You mow the lawn with that?!"

I blinked at him. "Yes."

"Our landscaper has a big thing that he just drives all over the property. But our yard isn't like yours. You have trees and stuff."

"I wasn't really paying attention to your yard," I said.

"You didn't miss anything. Other than the flower gardens it's basically green carpet." He bit his lower lip. "Do you think I could try it?"

"Try what? Pushing a lawnmower?"

"Yeah!" He had a greedy, kind of crazed look on his face.

"Do you have any chores at home?"

"Clean my room if we have company coming. Which is stupid since they don't go in my room anyway."

"I guess it couldn't hurt if you really want to."

He practically skipped as he ran to the shed.

"Hold this handle and pull back on the rip cord," I instructed.

It took him a few tries but when the engine roared to life, he cackled almost like a lunatic. I explained over the loud motor how to make passes over the grass. He obeyed and as I cleaned up the bigger pieces of debris, I heard him continue to laugh maniacally every time he ran over something that was mulched to bits. By early afternoon, the yard was practically immaculate.

I heard my stomach rumble. "You want some lunch?"

"Thank the Lord. I'm starved."

"Figure I can at least feed you for all the work you've done."

As we made our way into the house, I felt that twinge of embarrassment again. There were breakfast dishes still in the sink and a basket of unfolded laundry waiting for me in Daddy's recliner. The house wasn't dirty but it was untidy. I tried to gauge his body language as we entered the kitchen area. In my house, our kitchenette was very small but the joint dining space and living area was quite large and homey. He seemed to be looking around, taking in the small (compared to his house) space but I saw no signs of negative judgment. We washed our hands in the sink and dried them with paper towels. He then stood behind me with his hands in his pockets and watched as I collected bread, peanut butter, and plates from various cabinets and drawers. I felt his eyes on me as I prepared our meal and felt a little uncomfortable.

"Is something the matter?" I asked.

"No," he said. "Not at all."

"Well, then could you sit down? You're making me nervous," I said.

He chuckled a little. "I'd love to. I was always told you never sit in a house until you've been invited. I didn't want to show you any bad manners."

"I guess Daddy said that too at some point," I admitted. "But I never gave it much thought on account that I don't go anywhere or really visit anybody."

"Well," he said. "For future reference, you always have an open invitation to sit in my house."

I smiled at him. "Likewise."

I set a plate containing a peanut butter sandwich, corn chips, and two chocolate chip cookies in front of him and filled a glass of lemonade.

He picked up a cookie and examined it. "I've never seen cookies like this before."

"I made them myself," I said, feeling that bit of self-consciousness bubbling in my belly.

"You made these cookies?"

"Yes."

"I don't know that I've ever had a cookie that didn't come from the store," he admitted. "Martha always buys cookies at the grocery for me and the caterers always make fancy things like cakes and souffles so they don't bother with cookies."

I watched him grin like a small child as he ate his sandwich and corn chips and drank his lemonade. He then took a bite of his cookie. His eyes rolled back a little and he leaned back in his chair.

"These are so much better than store-bought," he smiled with crumbs still stuck on his lips.

"Well, I'm glad you like them," I said.

After lunch, we reclined in the kitchen chairs for a little and talked more about school and classes coming up in the fall. At around 4:00 he excused himself to go home for supper. After he left, I cleaned the dishes, folded the laundry, and prepared for supper when Daddy got home.

"Yard looks great, Peanut!" Daddy beamed as he came in.

"Thank you. Trey came out and helped me get it all done."

Daddy's face flattened. "That boy from the other day?"

"Yes," I said and continued to stir the pot of spaghetti sauce.

"What's his intentions?" Daddy asked.

I smiled. "I don't know," I said honestly. "I think I can call him a friend."

"Well, if he intends for more, he'd better come talk to me first."

I smiled in earnest. "Yes, Daddy."

It was another four days before Trey came to visit me again. I sat on the dock with my feet in the water throwing stale bread to the minnows. I heard the Lexus pull into the driveway and he got out. He came up and sat beside me and began to take his shoes and socks off to stick them in the water alongside mine.

"How's your week going?" he asked.

"Okay," I said. "Been doing a lot of reading."

"What are you reading?"

"Murder mystery," I said. "I think the wife did it but I feel like that's too obvious."

He wrinkled his nose. "It's not gory or anything is it?"

"No," I said. "Nothing like that." I lifted my foot out of the water. "What have you been doing this week?"

He leaned back on his palms and wiggled his toes under the water. "Mom and Dad just got back from California," he said. "Dad had some business meeting and Mom went to go shopping and spend a little time on the beach."

"Why didn't you get to go?" I questioned. I couldn't imagine Daddy taking a trip without me for business or otherwise.

He laughed a laugh completely devoid of happiness. "I don't usually get to go with them on their trips. They say they don't have time to make sure I'm staying out of trouble and they don't want to bring a nanny."

"Well, that doesn't sound right," I said. "How long are they home for?"

"They already left," he said. "This time it's just a short trip to shake some hands in New York. Then they'll be home for 2 weeks. Well, Mom will be home for 2 weeks and then she is heading to Georgia to spend some time with a friend of hers. Dad will be home for most of the rest of this summer but he's always in the office so I won't see him much."

"That's kind of sad," I admitted. "I don't get to see Daddy very much except on the weekends when he's home but at least he comes home for dinner every night."

"It's all right," he said. "I'll get a few dinners in with Dad, I think. Honestly, this is the way it's been my whole life so it's just what I'm used to." He took a slice of the stale bread that was sitting next to me and began throwing it out for the minnows. "Why are we feeding these little fish?"

"Everything has to eat and no sense in letting bread go to waste," I said.

"Got any chores that need to be done?"

"Nope," I said. "All done today."

"Want to go somewhere?"

"Like where?"

"I don't know. I'd like to go get some ice cream. It's awful hot today."

"We can go down to the Dairy Corner," I suggested.

"What's that?'

I looked at him in disbelief. "Only the best ice cream in the state of West Virginia," I said.

He grinned. "I'll be the judge of that."

We got up and dried off our feet with a towel sitting next to me. Along the way I told him all of the best flavors they offered. I pointed out where to go and he parked outside the little stand on the corner. There was hardly enough room for the two employees at the window. I got my favorite hand-dipped strawberry while he got one scoop of caramel swirl, one scoop of fudge swirl, and one scoop of peanut butter. I looked at his bowl and he smiled with the spoon hanging out of his mouth.

"Couldn't decide?" I asked.

"Nope."

We ate our ice cream and walked around the town. I pointed out my old elementary school and where the farmer's market set up on the weekends. He admitted that beyond the grocery store and the library he had never really spent much time in town. Because he was gone throughout the school year and his friends were all at school, he really didn't do much when he was at home besides play video games and harass Martha. When we finished our ice cream, I bought us sodas from the pony keg and we went to the park. He got a little too close to a Canadian goose and I saw just how fast a lacrosse player could run. I lay in the grass laughing and unable to help him. When the goose felt he had been sufficiently punished for his infraction, it returned to the flock and he came to find me still lying in the sun, still unable to breathe.

"Thanks for that," he said.

"I'm so sorry. I couldn't. You should have seen yourself!"

"Yeah," he said sitting down next to me. "I don't think I can blame you as much as I may want to."

He nudged me with his shoulder. I have to admit, the physical contact felt pretty good. He returned me home and it was another two or three days before we saw each other again. This time, he invited me to his house to play video games. I reluctantly agreed. The deeper into his house he led me, the more criminal it felt for me to be there. My sandals squeaked up the staircase, announcing to the whole house that there was an intruder.

I didn't realize the television and gaming system were in his bedroom. I had never been in a boy's bedroom before. Daddy would have a heart attack if he knew. I looked around at the perfectly made king-sized bed. I couldn't imagine having so much space to sleep. I was still sleeping on the twin-sized mattress that my parents had bought me when I was four years old. He had a small loveseat and a big squishy-looking chair sitting in front of the TV in the corner. He also had the standard dresser and nightstand. I didn't even want to ask how big his closet was. I looked around and took it all in.

"You tidied it up before I came over, didn't you?"

"Of course. I told you my one chore is to clean my room before a guest comes over."

I smiled and sat in the squishy-looking chair.

"Come sit next to me," he said, sitting in the roomy loveseat. I hesitated but did so. "Here, flip the switch on the side," he said. He pushed a button and the leg rest popped out.

I did the same. "I didn't even know sofas did this!"

He laughed and handed me a controller. "Come on. We're going to box each other," he said. "I owe you for that right hook a few weeks ago."

I beat him. Over and over and over. He mockingly scowled and called me a button masher. He said I had no actual skill it was all luck. I told him of course it was because I had never played that game before in my life. After a few hours, I became bored. I asked him if we could go outside. We went out and wandered through his lawn. He wasn't joking about the lawn looking like a green carpet. There was not a dandelion or purple clover to be seen. It was edged with beautiful flower beds and there was a large weeping willow taking center stage in the middle of the yard. We stood under it and I looked up.

"How many times have you climbed it?" I asked him.

"I've never climbed a tree," he said.

I shook my head. "Every time you say something, I feel more pity for you." I grabbed ahold of a low-hanging branch and swung my leg over it. I stood on that branch, grabbed the next one, and hoisted myself up. "Come on!"

He bounced a little bit before grabbing a branch and mimicking what I had done. We climbed as high as we dared and looked out over the property.

"There's so much here but so little," I said.

He nodded. "We've got about forty acres but that includes the part of the lake that we own and the trees around it. But what's around the house really isn't much. Not like your land. How much do you guys have?"

"Seven acres," I said. "But it's all woods. You saw how tiny my little yard is."

"I'd rather have that tiny little lawn and big woods than all this space with nothing to do with it."

A few days later he returned again. This time he asked for my phone number so he could talk to me when he wasn't able to come visit. I told him sure but it was a landline phone number. I didn't have my own cell phone and I was rarely in the house in the summer. He said that was fine. He would like the number anyway so he might get lucky and reach me when I was inside. He also asked for my email address. I felt a little apprehensive but provided it. That defined the rest of our summer. We did chores at my house or went into town for ice cream, perused the library, and spent time at the park.

We spent some time at his house, much to Martha's dismay. She still hadn't forgiven me for bleeding all over the entryway floor. I didn't like being inside his house anyway. I always felt like I didn't belong there and one day the house was just going to vomit me out of its own accord. We played ball and threw a frisbee in the big open space of his yard where I felt more comfortable. He tried to teach me how to catch the way he did in Lacrosse but my hand-eye coordination was just not good enough for that. On the days we couldn't spend time together, we corresponded mostly through email. I still hadn't met his parents but it was fair because he still hadn't met Daddy.

When it came time for him to go back to school at the end of summer, he promised to write to me every day. I didn't believe him and chalked it up to a summertime friendship. But he was true to his word. He emailed me sometimes even three times in a day. Kelly giggled and accused me of being in a long-distance relationship. I didn't believe anything romantic was transpiring between us. All I knew was I was happy to open my email every day.

At Christmas time, I got a package in the mail. It was a pretty red sweater that was softer than anything I had ever felt. The card said he had picked it out himself and he hoped I liked it. I trudged through the cold up to his house the next day and handed Martha a package and asked her to make sure he got it. She sneered and touched the box with just two fingers. Three days later I got an email about how my cookies had made him the envy of all of his friends.

The following summer I got a part-time job at the Dairy Corner scooping ice cream. On my second day of work, I got a request for caramel swirl, fudge swirl, and peanut butter in the same bowl. I smiled at the handsome blue-eyed blonde boy in front of me. His hair was a little thicker and his shoulders were a little broader.

He smiled at me. "You look good," he said. "What days are you here?"

"Tuesdays and Thursdays," I said.

He nodded. "I'll see you at your house tomorrow then," he said.

That summer went much the way the previous one had. We continued to email every day and made time to see each other where we could. That fall I bought a used car off of one of Daddy's friends. I slid on some ice my first winter driving and had to walk three miles in the snow to get back home. Daddy panicked and got me a cell phone. After that, we spoke on the phone every single day. I didn't think Daddy knew how close Trey and I were becoming at all and I wanted to keep it that way. The only person who knew was Kelly and she giggled and poked fun at me for it every chance she got.

In April during spring break, I was invited to Trey's house for a birthday party. I did the best I could to fix my hair and donned the sweater he had bought me two Christmases before. When I showed up at the door, Martha let me in and Trey stood there beaming. I looked around with the video game I had wrapped for him in my hand.

"Where is everyone else?" I asked.

"It's just us. I'm so glad you came."

"What do you mean it's just us?"

"Dad had to fly out yesterday and took Mom with him. Since the other guests were all their friends, they all sent their gifts," he gestured to the sideboard that was laden with wrapped packages. "But no one else is coming."

"None of your friends from school?" I asked. "Eighteen is kind of a big deal."

He shrugged. "They would have to fly in and most of their parents didn't want to pay for it," he admitted.

I couldn't control myself. I wrapped my arms around his shoulders and squeezed him tight. He pulled me into himself and buried his face in the top of my head.

"Happy birthday," I said into his chest.

"Thanks, Sarah. You have no idea how much it means to me that you are here."

That was four months ago. Two weeks ago, we went to the fair. We shot pellet guns at balloons and played the squirt gun game. We watched the tractor pull and watched the kids get their 4-H animals judged. We ate cotton candy and elephant ears and honestly far more sugar than anyone should. The night topped off with a ride on the merry-go-round. I felt like a little kid again as the wind rushed past my face. He held on to his pony and smiled at me.

After he took me home, he walked me to the door. He kissed me on the lips. It was my first kiss. I had no idea what I was doing but I knew how right it felt.

"I love you," he said to me.

My heart stopped. My throat choked. I had not expected that at all.

"I love you too," I squeaked.

He smiled broadly and kissed me again.

The next day he called me and asked if he could call on my house at suppertime so he could meet Daddy. I felt sick. I could actually tell my skin had turned green and my stomach became a bubbling cauldron of acid but I knew it had to be done. I steadied my nerves as best I could by scrubbing the house from top to bottom. I set the table and tried to fold the napkins as fancy as I could find on the internet. I tried swans at first but that was a failure so I settled for a fan. I washed and dressed and put the lasagna in the oven just in time for Daddy to get home.

He looked around and whistled. "What's all this then?"

"Daddy?" I could hear the fear in my own voice.

His face fell. "Yes?"

"Remember that thing you made me promise you about Trey?"

"Oh." Daddy's eyes popped and he stepped back a little. "All right then. Let me go get cleaned up."

Daddy showered and came out with his hair slicked back and his face cleanly shaven. He sat at the table with only a few minutes to spare before there was a knock at the door. He stood, smoothed his pants, and looked at me. I was standing in the kitchenette, biting my nails. He opened it.

"Mr. Crittenden?" Trey stood on the other side. He was dressed nicely in a button-down shirt and even wore a tie for the occasion.

"That'd be me," Daddy said.

"My name is Trey Sherman." He held his hand out for Daddy to shake.

"Good to finally meet you." Daddy shook his hand.

I felt a breath I didn't realize I had been holding escape me and I became a little dizzy. I served lasagna and bread and throughout the meal, Daddy interrogated Trey about school and sports and his plans for college in the fall. Trey admitted he had been accepted to a school in Maryland and was going to study business as his father had before him.

"And what about my daughter being back here?" Daddy asked.

"Well," Trey said. "I've been going away to school every fall so far and I don't see that college is going to be much different."

"You realize college is a lot more work than just high school, right?"

Trey smiled weakly. "Yes, sir. But I love your daughter."

"I know it," Daddy said. "She thought she was being sneaky adding her own minutes to the phone. I know who she's been talking to all this time." I felt my face redden. "But teenage love is one thing. Starting a life together is another."

"Dad," I said solemnly. "Daddy we ain't talking about getting married."

Trey bit his lower lip.

"I know you two are in love. But I know that love is hard when you put it under pressure. Right now, you two have been running all over West Virginia doing your own thing with no pressure. But when you both are expected to perform at school -- and Peanut, when you go off to college next year God only knows where -- are you guys going to be able to make it work being separated so far for so long?"

"We won't know unless we try," Trey said.

"I respect that." Daddy nodded. "I really do. But I have to protect my little girl. And I know she's going to get her heart broken. You two are from two different worlds. And you're going to have expectations put on you that she may not measure up to," Daddy said.

I felt my lower lip tremble and my eyes burned a little bit. I knew what Daddy was saying and I think a part of me knew Daddy was right but I didn't want to admit that. Above all else, I knew that I loved Trey.

"I understand what you're saying sir," Trey said. "And I cannot predict how I will react in certain situations but I can say that I like to believe that I am man enough to do the right thing and I know in my heart right now the right thing is doing what's right for your daughter."

"Are you sure this is what's right for my daughter?"

"Yes."

Daddy sighed. "Well, all right then. I have to respect an honest man." He stood and held his hand out for Trey to shake. Trey shook it firmly. "You all have my blessing, whatever may happen."

I smiled and the burning in my eyes from tears of hurt turned into a burning from tears of happiness. I had Daddy's blessing. That night, as I lay in bed after Trey had kissed me goodnight, I heard Daddy's words replay in my head. Trey and I are from two different worlds. Hadn't Trey himself once said that 'with certain status comes certain expectations?' I know he was only quoting his own father, but there was truth to that statement. I was average. I didn't have the grace and elegance of the women in his social circles.

Two days later I was invited to supper at the Sherman Estate to meet Trey's parents. I must have showered at least four times that day. I tried on every outfit I had from the sweater he had bought me to the dress I kept mainly for funerals. I finally settled on a pink dress that I had forgotten I even owned and wasn't sure how long it had been since I'd worn it. I fought with my hair for at least an hour and broke down into frustrated tears.

When I arrived, Trey met me at the door. He was smiling broadly and he looked so handsome. He escorted me into what they called the sitting room. His parents stood.

"Mom, Dad, this is Sarah Crittenden. Sarah, these are my parents, Steven and Autumn Sherman."

Steven was tall, lean, and had salt-and-pepper hair. He wore a blue sweater over a white shirt and brown pants. Autumn had long movie-star-blonde hair, like her son's, flowing down behind a pink and white floral sundress. Her lips were full and pink and there was not a single crack or line to be seen in her skin.

I shook his father's hand first. When I reached to shake his mother's hand, she stuck one highly manicured fingernail underneath my chin and used it to guide my face from side to side. "She could be very pretty with a little bit of work," she said.

"Mom!"

"What?"

Martha appeared and announced that dinner would be served in the dining hall. Trey put his hand on the small of my back and led me from the room as his father did the same with his mother. He pulled a chair out for me to be seated before seating himself. It was the most awkward dinner table I had ever been at. His father sat at the head of the table. To his left, three seats down on the side sat Trey. I sat next to Trey. There were then two empty seats next to me with his mother seated at the other head of the table. I could not imagine having so much separation for a family meal.

His father began talking business with him while his mother tried to engage me in conversation about fashion and travel and things I had no interest in or understanding. Towards the end of the meal, everything switched over and his dad started trying to talk to me about my plans for college and my intentions for my future.

At the end of supper, he sighed. "Sarah," he said. "You seem like a very lovely girl. But I don't think this is a good match."

"Dad, I didn't bring her here to ask if it was a good match. I wanted you to meet the woman I love," Trey said.

"I understand that. I really do. But love is only part of the equation."

"What else matters?" Trey asked.

"A good wife is more than just emotional support," his mother said. "Look at all the things I do for your father. I go to boring business dinners and play nice with his partners' wives. I put a lot of effort into my appearance so that I look good because if I look good, your father looks good. Sarah, sweetie, I just don't see you being able to uplift Trey the way he's going to need if he's going to be successful."

"I don't want to marry you," Trey looked at his mother with, what I think, was little hatred. There was an edge to his voice that I had never heard before. "I love Sarah. *If* we marry someday then so be it but I like how she makes me feel and I think we are good for each other and I don't think anything else matters."

"That's adorable," his mother said. "But you're an adult now. And you need to start thinking about your adult future. Sarah is not accustomed to our way of life and, well, you know what they say about teaching an old dog new tricks. I'm sure we could make her into something presentable but at the end of the day, I don't know that she will fit in with your plans for the future if you are going to follow in your father's footsteps."

I swallowed hard. I wasn't going to cry in front of them. I refused to. I had never heard such hateful things said about me and the fact that they were probably right made it hurt even more.

Trey stood and held his hand out to me. "Come on, Sarah. I don't feel that we are welcome at this table anymore," he said. He escorted me out the front door and we stood beside one of the massive white pillars. "I am so sorry," he said.

"What if they're right?"

"What do you mean?"

I felt a tear fall down my right cheek. "Both Daddy and your parents said the same thing. We're from two different worlds. I want to be a doctor. I can't do what your mom does and travel all over the place to be there for you. 'With certain status comes certain expectations.'"

"And like I said," he said sternly. "That's not what I want. I don't want their life."

"But like you said," I looked up into his beautiful blue eyes. "It's the only life you've ever known. Could you really be happy without a maid and having to do chores every day and living in a tiny little house like the one I live in with Daddy?"

He chewed on the inside of his cheek before he answered. "I'd have to learn," he said.

"Or I'd have to learn how to live like this." I gestured at the mansion. "How do we decide? Even if your mom made me into something presentable, they've made it clear that they will never accept me."

"What are you saying?" he asked.

"I'm saying I need to think," I admitted.

I leaned up and kissed him on the cheek and squeezed his hand. I would not allow myself to look back at him as I backed out of the driveway and drove home, sobbing the entire way. I could not bring myself to answer his phone call the next day. Or the next. I could not stop hearing his parents and Daddy in my head. I could not ignore how out of place I felt every time I stepped foot in his house. I felt like asking him to live with less was asking him to give up his whole life. On the third day, he showed up at my house.

"Will you at least talk to me?" he asked.

I nodded and opened the screen door for him to come in. Tom immediately began making figure eights between his ankles.

"Don't tell me you let what they said get to you."

"But they're right," I said.

"What do you mean 'they're right?'"

"You want to go off to business school and I want to go off to medical school and even if we made it work staying together while we're in school what happens afterwards? Do we get an apartment? Where are we going to live? Have you even lived in something so small?" I asked.

"The dorms at school are pretty small," he said, trying to force a smile.

"Trey," I said.

"What? So, you don't even want to try?"

"I don't know that I can," I admitted. "The longer we stay together, the more it's going to hurt if we don't make it."

"*If.* You said it yourself," he said. "*If.*"

I looked down at my hands.

"So that's it then?"

I nodded. "I think so."

"Then, okay," he turned on his heel and stormed out, slamming the screen door open behind him.

I cried. I cried for two days. Kelly told me I was stupid and foolish. I had a wonderful person who was willing to change his whole life for me and I threw it all away. Daddy backed up my decision, however. He said he knew it hurt now but it was better than the hurt I would feel years down the road if we even made it that far. But I thought about how he had stood up to Martha and his parents for me. How he had treated me like his equal from day one. How he had never questioned my house, that was all me. I just wanted to hear his voice one more time. So, I called. He didn't answer. I called the next day. He didn't answer. I sent him an email explaining that I was stupid and begging him to talk to me. But he didn't answer. That was it. That was days ago and he is now in Maryland.

And here I sit. Alone with my feet in the water. Wishing. Wishing things could go back to the way they were. Wondering how did this ever work before I broke it. At least Romeo and Juliet died quickly whereas I feel I may die from this broken heart.

Chapter 2

Remember

Remember you are loved.
　　Remember someone cares.
Even when it feels as if
no one else is there.
Remember to be strong.
Remember you are tough,
even when just getting up
feels a little rough.
Remember those who mock
and laugh behind your back
aren't worth the time of day.
It's empathy they lack.
Remember what you're fighting for,
be it beast or kin.
All the strength you feel you lost
is tightly sealed within.
Remember who you are,
yourself, not another.
If you dare forget these things
your soul cannot recover.

Chapter 3

Seek truth

Moon bright,
    soft light.
Heaven is looking down.
I see the soul
of Earth untold and
Death speaks Silent Sound.
I know not what
ought to be
and Love
should freely fly.
It is not
the way
of the world they say
as death shall tell us lies.

Chapter 4

Addiction

She is my drug of choice. Junkies can keep their heroin and meth. This Venus is true addiction. Call it obsession or infatuation if you must. In truth, it is far more than that. Authors and poets have written of love and beauty for millennia, but no sonnet over composed could accurately describe her or how she made me feel.

Her skin was visibly soft and her legs were long and lean. Her hair was a ginger-colored river that flowed from her angelic pate. And her scent... there are no words. I would scour the globe to find a way to bottle that scent and keep it for myself. The sweet airiness- something like a peony- would linger in a room after she had left. I would stand in her place and breathe her in. That was a high that drug users would spend a lifetime chasing. On the days she didn't come into work, when I couldn't hear the melody of her voice or smell her sweetness, I felt physical pain. My heart would hurt and I couldn't catch my breath. I would spend sleepless nights praying to the Gods to end my suffering until I could breathe her in again.

Every morning, I would make sure I arrived to work before her to set up the coffee just the way she liked it. It had to be one-third of a cup of regular, one-third of a cup of French roast, and one-fourth of a cup of sugar added with the grounds in the filter so it would melt evenly through the whole pot. I would also wipe my name off of her favorite vanilla creamer that I kept stocked in the fridge. I would only share with her and, when she wasn't looking, write my name back on it in dry erase maker so that no one but her could use it.

Every morning, I would asker her, "How's the coffee, Ellie?"

Every morning, she would answer, "Best part of my day, Alastor."

I was the best part of her day.

After work, I would follow her little green Focus in my little black Camry. I made sure to stay at a distance. She didn't need to be worrying about me the way I worried about her. Other drivers on the road were dangerous and I couldn't live with myself if I knew anything bad had befallen her. It was forty minutes in the opposite direction from my house, but she was single and lived alone. There was no one else to protect her.

Sometimes, at night, I would get up and drive to her house and sit out front and watch her windows to reassure myself that she was okay. I would sit and smile and dream that I was in that house with her, that I was laying in her sheets and breathing her in through the night. Elandra Asher. Could you, one day, be Elandra Huxley? Could you, Ellie? Would you one day take my name as you have taken my heart and mind? I will gladly give it to you. I will give you anything you desire if you will let me feel the softness of your skin and the silk of your hair. Without you in my life at all, I would be nothing. I would shrivel and die.

One cold winter day, she was having her morning coffee and chatting with Jacob. I don't like Jacob. He shamelessly flirted with her but she was too naïve to see through his ruse. But I wasn't. I was careful to keep a protective eye on her whenever he was around. I was standing nearby drinking my tea- white so the odor was not too strong- and listening while I got my 'fix' of her fragrance.

"I hope my cat forgives me for leaving for two weeks." She sighed. "She hates boarding at the kennel but I don't want to give just anyone a key to my house, you know?"

I choked a little on my tea. *Two weeks? She would be gone for two weeks?!*

Jacob looked up at me and shook his head. He turned his attention back to her. "Where, exactly, are you going again?"

"Pasadena. My family is there and I really miss them. And I miss California weather in these awful Indiana winters."

"Makes sense. When do you leave, again?"

"Saturday morning. I appreciate you taking me to the airport. That's still okay, right?"

"Of course! Always glad to do a friend a favor."

Saturday? That's the day after tomorrow. And HE is going to take you to the airport!

I felt sick. I set my mug on the counter in the break room and left. What was I going to do? I couldn't be without her for two weeks! I'd die of withdrawal! I went to the men's room and vomited my tea into the sink.

I barely slept that night and I didn't sleep at all Friday night. Just the thought of not seeing her for TWO WEEKS was almost too much to bear. On Saturday morning, I parked my car a few houses down the street from her house and watched. Here came Jacob from the opposite end of the street. He was easy to spot in his flashy red F150. There was salt and sand on the roads to keep them from freezing, but his truck was immaculately clean. He probably washed it just to impress her. What a prick.

I watched him hop out, straighten his coat, and knock on the door. Through my binoculars I could see her door open and she invited him in with a perfect smile. That lucky bastard was in her house. He was surrounded by everything that smelled like her. He was touching all of the things that had been touched by her. He was standing on the carpet that she walked upon and

I'll bet he had no appreciation for any of it. His only goal was in her bedroom and this 'favor' was just a steppingstone to get him there.

A few minutes later I watched her door open and he carried out her carry-on bag and wheeled out a suitcase. He plopped them in the back seat of the cab and rushed to the other side of the truck. She locked her door, gave her garage a tug, and met him beside the truck. He opened the passenger door and helped her in. I watched them drive off together into the horizon pink.

By Monday I wanted to die. I tried to go to work but I hadn't slept for nearly four days. I was so unbearably sick from it that I couldn't keep down any food. There was a gaping void where my heart should have been and someone had parked a truck on my chest. My sallow skin and blackened eyes gave Cecil cause for concern, so he sent me home.

I lay on my couch all afternoon. I begged for death. No such sweet release would come. I couldn't take the pain anymore. I gathered up as much of my strength as I could and drove to her house. I had to find some sort of relief. It was cold and well past midnight. I got out of my car and walked up to her bright blue front door. I wasn't likely to be seen and I didn't care if I was. I couldn't go on like this and she needed me to protect her.

I walked around the outside of the house and peeked into the darkened windows. I don't know what I was looking for, but I found something. She lived in one of the older homes in the area that had the original stone foundation basements. There were windows that had been added a little later but I could clearly see through the clear plastic window well cover that one of the windows was broken. I carefully and as quietly as I could broke the plastic loose.

Maybe...

I hadn't kept any food down in four days. I might just fit. Was I really going to do this? Was I really going to break into her home while she was out of town? I felt a horrible pain in my chest.

Yes.

I took off my coat, lay on my chest, and slid down through the window. I'd worry about the plastic later. It was dark down there but I used the light of my cell phone to find the stairs. They were steep and slick from condensation. When I found the door at the top, I entered into the main floor of the house. I found a light switch on a nearby wall and flipped it. A light came on in the basement below me. I flipped the switch next to that one.

When the room lit up, it was everything I'd imagined it would be and more. The tiny kitchen at the back of the house had a big double French door that led out to the patio. The walls were a soft yellow and the little round café-style table was just big enough for two. I followed the white tile until it met carpet in the living room.

I turned on the lamp. Her couch had a pink floral pattern; a little girlier than I expected. The walls were a barely-there shade of tan and the carpet was a little darker brown. My footsteps didn't make a sound as I continued.

I passed the bathroom on the right. It was perfect and clean as I expected it to be. But the room at the end of the hall...that was her bedroom. I could see into it when she would undress after work sometimes. I knew the walls were blue but as I stepped foot into it for the first time, a flood of emotion came over me. It was a small room. The carpet was the same light tan as the living room. On the dresser was a hairbrush. I picked it up and ran my fingers over the silken threads it held. I took a deep breath. I was completely surrounded by her smell and it was amazing. I collapsed onto the blue floral bedspread, still clutching the brush.

The next thing I knew was morning. I had kicked off my shoes sometime in the night and completely passed out. I called

Cecil and told him I still wasn't well and was taking the day off. I spent the entire day sleeping on that bedspread. Every breath I took smelled of her. I could feel my whole soul healing.

By three in the morning on Wednesday, I had a new pain. I was hungry for the first time in a week. I decided to get food and make an appearance at work and I'd return later. I went back through the house to exit the same way I had come in. I didn't have a key, after all.

Now, here I am, in that basement and forced to stare at the lightbulb dangling above my head. It flickers. On. Off. On. Off. Dim. Bright. Off. Swinging from a chain just above my head. Dim. Off. Bright. I can't reach it to unscrew the infernal glass. Bright. Off. Bright. Dim. Its motion and flickering is casting dancing shadows on the damp walls. I watch them and wonder if anyone will find me here. Will they find my body or my bones? Maybe she'll come home early and save me. Bright. Off. No. This isn't television and no one will rescue me just in the nick of time. I will lay here with my foot next to my ear. My leg and back and who knows what else are broken. Dim. Bright. Dim.

I didn't realize just how slippery the cellar stairs would be. As I came crashing down, my leg slipped on the wet stone. Down I went, somehow snapping that very leg. I don't feel it, though. When I landed, the edge of one of the steps caught me in the back. It hurt at first, when my vertebrae separated. But that was (I think) two or three days ago. I haven't felt anything below my ribs in quite some time. It's dark down here other than the incessant flickering. Dim. Bright. Dim. I was hungry. That's what led me down here but my stomach gave up that fight. I had tried to pull myself out, but my right arm is dislocated from trying to stop my fall down the stairs.

So here I lay. Trapped. Probably laying in my own waste. All I can think of is her. Will she suffer without me as I have suffered without her? Every breath has been progressively difficult. I can-

not swallow and my tongue is dry and swollen. Each breath...
Dim. Bright. Dim. Off.

Chapter 5

Written in my Sleep at 430am

I just want to preface this by saying I have no idea where it came from. I woke up out of a dead sleep at 430 in the morning to write it for some reason. I don't feel like it's my best work but clearly my unconscious brain felt it needed to be shared.

You think you've won
but at what cost?
Look at all
the lives you lost.
Your wife now with
another man.
Your ring missing
from her hand.
Daughter's not looked
your way in years.
Last you saw
she was in tears.
Your son's like you,
put money first.
Won't be a dad.
Thinks you're the worst.
Your mom has died.

You missed the wake
for a meeting
you had to take.
Who needs friends?
You have peers.
Relationships die
after some years.
Alone you sit
with work to do.
Your money there
to fulfil you.
No time for love.
No time for fun.
Kinship forfeit.
Wealth has won.

Chapter 6

Soulmates

Oh, what light!
Heaven's soft glow
bear down on mortals
into the throw.

The pure song
has been sung.
Cannot circumvent
the human lung.

Oh beauty!
Much to see!
Glory of my heart,
listen to me!

We are one
of our minds
and also our souls.
Always entwined.

Chapter 7

Overwhelmed

People. People
  everywhere
wearing bright colors.
Moving fast.
Moving close.
People. People.
Hear them speak.
Why breathe so loud?
Laughing.
Shoes Clicking.
People. People
making smells.
Breath when they speak.
Body odors.
Perfume odors.
People. People
shake my hand.
Crowding all around.
Touch my back.
Trod my foot.
People. People.
Cannot think.
Nowhere to hide.

Cannot breathe.
Closing in.

Chapter 8

A Little Love Poem

Strong but smart.
　　Sweet and kind.
How is it
that you are mine?

Skin like satin.
Hair like silk.
Hold you close.
Drink you as milk.

Soul so pure.
Heart so full.
Your nature
cannot be cruel.

Come to me
my sweet beau.
Come join me
and know no woe.

Chapter 9

The Truth Shall Set You Free

Her hair was obsidian black and as shiny and perfect as cornsilk. Donnie loved her hair. It had been the first thing he'd noticed about her. She had had it piled high on her head and, as she stood with her back to him in the market, she removed a clip and it fell like a silk curtain down her back. Donnie was mesmerized by its perfection. He longed to touch it. He reached his hand out but stopped himself. He realized he was no longer in the market. He was in a room, surrounded by men and women in suits and one in a black robe sat next to him. He wasn't looking at the beautiful woman, but a picture of her that was held in front of him.

"Mr. Evans?" the man holding the picture asked.

"I'm sorry. Yes. Yes, I've seen her before," Donnie answered.

"Could you tell the courtroom where that might have been? Tell the truth." the man said.

"Yes. At the farmers market, I think."

"Let the record show," the man said, "that the defendant has confirmed and acknowledged visual contact with Ms. Olivia Kincaid." He set the picture down and turned back to Donnie. "Mr. Evans, did you speak with Ms. Kincaid?"

"Yes."

"What did you say?"

"Excuse me."

"I asked what you said to Ms. Kincaid."

"That is what I said." Donnie shifted in the uncomfortable chair. "I said 'excuse me.'"

Donnie thought back, again, to that day. It had been warm and the sun had been high. It reflected off of her perfect hair like a shining black mirror. He had been walking behind her and when she stopped to look at a table of handmade soaps, his attention was attracted to a variety of infused honeys at the table across the sidewalk. They had both turned after making their purchases and bumped into each other.

"And that's when I said, 'excuse me,'" Donnie finished recounting his story.

"Did she say something back?" the prosecutor pressed.

"She said something like, um," Donnie looked up as he thought as if expecting it to be printed on his brain for him to see. "'No. It's my fault. I'm sorry.'" Donnie nodded satisfactorily at his recollection.

"Is that all?"

"Yes."

"You said nothing else to her for the rest of the day?"

"No, sir."

"Did you see Ms. Kincaid at all for the rest of the day?"

Donnie scratched the back of his neatly trimmed, honey-colored hair. "Must've. Farmer's market isn't that big a place. I'm almost positive I saw her in the parking lot before I left."

"Almost certain?"

"Yes."

"Mr. Evans, were you, at any point, following Ms. Kincaid?"

Donnie remembered seeing her with a little girl. The child had a sign that she was braiding hair for two dollars so that she could earn money for a bicycle. A woman, Donnie assumed to be her mother, was selling potted plants at the table next to her and engaging the little girl's clients in conversation. She had just finished braiding the long, stringy, pewter hair of a biker in worn black cuts when the exquisite black-haired woman sat in front of her. The girl carefully, but not very skillfully, created a plait down the woman's back. She polished her work with a red pygmy rose from her mother's table. The effect was innocent and pure.

Donnie locked eyes with the prosecutor. "Possible. Foot traffic at the market flows mostly in one direction.'

"But you are claiming it wasn't a conscious effort."

"That's a fair way to put it, yes. I was moving with the flow of people."

"How, then, do you explain Ms. Kincaid's hairs that were found in your car?"

"I just told you I bumped into her. I must have gotten some of her hairs on me and they came off in the car."

"They were in the back seat."

"I had put the potted rose I'd bought and the big jar of honey, the kind with the comb still in it, in my backseat."

"What is the color, make, and model of your vehicle?"

"I drive a silver Toyota Prius."

"You are aware that Ms. Olvia Kincaid's next-door neighbor has testified that she saw a silver Prius drive passed her home that afternoon and then drive away down the street later after dark?"

"Yes. I'm also aware that I do not own the only silver Prius in Ohio."

A few of the twelve people to Donnie's left sniggered.

"If it wasn't you driving passed the Kincaid residence, where were you after you had left the market?"

"I went home and repotted my new plants. I had some dinner and watched some TV."

"Can anyone corroborate this?"

"The police took my neighbor's security camera footage. It shows what time I got home."

"But not that you stayed there."

"No. But my car didn't leave and from what I understand, it would have been quite a walk to her house."

The prosecutor, Martin Crosby, was a tall, pudgy man with thinning sandy hair. Donnie saw him clench his teeth. Martin knew Donnie was right, but he didn't have a rebuttal. He had known it was going to be a tough case to try and Donnie was smarter than he had anticipated. Calmly, he walked to a table and returned with a plastic bag.

"Can you identify these?" he asked.

Donnie squinted at the bag. "Those are my boots."

"Please note, that the defendant has identified them as *his* boots. These boots had mud on them consistent with the mud around the creek that's behind the defendant's house. Mud where drag marks were clearly visible when investigators went back there. Can you explain that, Mr. Evans?"

"Yes. I canoe in that creek and go fishing. It leads to the Little Miami River. Of course, there are drag marks and mud on my boots."

"Isn't it possible that they could be from you dragging Ms. Kincaid's body to the water to dispose of it?'

The prosecutor was interrupted by a tall, thin woman with long, blonde hair in a blue business suit.

"Objection," Donnie's defense said. "Speculation. Olivia Kincaid's body has not been found. For all we know the prosecutor himself cut her into pieces that are currently in a landfill."

The look Martin gave Bridget Tucker could have set her on fire.

"Sustained," the judge said.

Matin Crosby was visibly more agitated. "No further questions."

"Ms. Tucker?" the judge asked.

"No questions, your honor."

"The defendant may step down.'

Donnie got up from the uncomfortable chair. As he walked towards his attorney, she gave him a subtle smile and almost imperceptible nod.

"We call Adam O'Donell to the stand," Mr. Crosby announced.

The hair on the back of Donnie's neck stood on end as he watched the obese man who had squeezed into a too-small suit sit in the chair he had previously occupied. The chair groaned under his weight and the red-faced man puffed as he sat as if the twenty feet he had walked was nearly a marathon. He was sworn in and tugged gently as his green tie.

"Mr. O'Donell. Where were you on July seventeenth, 2021?"

"At the farmer's market down on Castle Rock Road."

"What did you see that you discussed with the police?"

"Donnie," Adam pointed at Donnie's chest, "watching a pretty lady with black hair in the parking lot."

Donnie thought back. He vaguely remembered seeing Adam standing near a truck as he loaded his flowers, honey, and assorted other purchases into the back seat of his car. More clearly, he remembered seeing that shining black plait kissing the small of Olivia's back and realizing he was close enough to her to walk up and introduce himself, but he had been too shy.

"There were a lot of people at the market that day," Martin Crosby stated. "Why do you remember that so clearly?"

"I didn't like the way he was looking at her." Adam glowered at Donnie as he said it.

"Could you elaborate?"

"It was kind of lustful. Predatory."

"How did the way he was looking at her make you feel?"

"I was concerned for her safety."

"Did you do anything as a result of that concern?"

"I stayed in the parking lot by my truck until they both left."

"So, you believe that, from what you witnessed, Mr. Evans intended to harm Ms. Kincaid?" Martin turned and faced the jury.

"No doubt in my mind," Adam stated succinctly.

The prosecutor cocked a smug grin. "Your witness."

Bridget Tucker stood and matched Martin's satisfactory smile.

"Mr. O'donell. How was it that you are so clearly able to identify my client, Donald Evans?'

"I've known him since we were kids," Adam shifted in his seat and the chair groaned in protest.

"So, you have a history with each other?"

"It's a small area." Adam narrowed his already piggy eyes. "Most folks know each other and other than the tourists, it's always the same people at the farmer's market every weekend."

"I'm not making myself clear." Bridget's voice oozed poison sweetness. "I mean the two of you have a *history*. You've never really gotten along with my client, even when you were children, did you?"

"No." The word was icy and sharp.

"As a matter of fact, you slashed his tires not long after you got out of high school, is that correct?"

"He ruined my football scholarship. He took everything from me! Now look at me!" Adam grabbed his protruding belly with both hands and shook it."

"Did you, or did you not, slash Mr. Evans's tires and serve community service for vandalism?"

"Damn right, I did."

"So, your negative feelings towards my client have not changed?"

"Not one bit."

"So then, is it possible, you are fabricating this story out of your hatred?"

"Objection!" The prosecutor stood.

"I'll allow it. Please answer the question." The judge motioned to Adam.

"No," he said through gritted teeth. "I know what I saw."

"Okay, then. You know what you saw." Bridget began pacing in front of him. "Did you see my client approach Olivia Kincaid?"

"No."

"Did you see him speak to or shout at her?'

"No."

"Did you see him do anything malicious besides *look* at her?"

"It was the way he looked at her."

"Please answer the question."

Adam was beet red and his eyes showed nothing but hatred toward the gorgeous blonde.

"No," he finally said.

"As a matter of fact, who did you see leave the parking lot first?"

There was an unmistakable set in Adam's jaw. "Donnie."

"On foot or in his car?"

"Car."

"So, you saw him leave first which means you did *not* see him follow her."

"No."

"No, you didn't see him follow her or no, I am incorrect?'

"No. I did not see him follow her."

"So. You did not see my client, a man you openly dislike and have committed crimes against, approach Olivia Kincaid. You did not see him talk to her. You did not see him interact with her in any way. You did *not* see him follow her because you *did* see him leave first." Bridget leaned forward and smiled. "But you saw him look at her." She said in almost a hushed, mocking tone. "No further questions."

Donnie saw Adam's hands ball into meaty fists. For a moment, he feared for Bridget's safety. The bailiff, sensing the same thing, grew rigid and ready to step in.

"You may step down," the judge said.

Adam puffed back to his seat, red and angry. Some of the twelve shook their heads while others made notes on little yellow pads.

"The prosecution calls Elise Evans." There was a note of discontent in Martin's voice at having his witness so discredited.

Donnie's heart stopped. His chest tightened. He couldn't breathe. He had not seen his cousin Elise in nearly fifteen years.

Forward stepped a stunning, pale woman. She wore a black pantsuit with a crisp, white blouse. Her high-heeled boots clicked as she walked across the tile floor. In high contrast to her very opalescent skin, long strands of shiny, black silk flowed behind her as she moved quickly to take her seat. Despite holding her head high and her jaw clenched, there was an unmistakable glint of fear in her eyes.

Elise was sworn in and seated. Donnie tried to take his eyes off of her but couldn't. They roved over every inch of her beauty. She sat stiff and intentionally not returning his gaze.

"Thank you for agreeing to come speak with us, Ms. Evans. I know this was difficult for you," Martin said gently. She nodded quickly and he continued. "Can you tell us how you are related to the defendant?"

"He, um..." she cleared her throat. "He is my cousin. His mom was my dad's sister."

"Was?"

"She died. About eight years ago."

"Were you and Donald Evans close growing up?"

Elise chewed her lip a little. "Not by choice."

"Could you explain what you mean for the court?"

She took a deep breath and let it out slowly. "Whenever his mom would disappear, he would come stay at our house. No one knows who his dad is so he couldn't take care of him. My sister and I were told to treat him like a brother."

"What do you mean she would 'disappear?'"

"Aunt Susan had Borderline Personality Disorder. She would run off with strange men or sometimes just run off in general. Sometimes for months at a time. Twice for over a year. She was at a psychiatric treatment facility for seventeen months and he lived with us then, too. She had inherited the farmhouse when Grams died so she always had a home to come back to."

"How did your parents feel about taking care of the defendant?'

"Dad always hated it. He says he spent their whole lives cleaning up after her messes and he listened to us when my sister, Neve, and I said Donnie made us uncomfortable. Mom didn't' though. Mom has always adored Donnie. Felt bad for him. She dotes on him still."

Seeing his opportunity, Martin's eyes brightened. "You said your sister and you felt uncomfortable with Donald Evans. Can you explain that?"

Elise seemed to be struggling to keep her composure. "When we were little, he would play Beauty Shop with us. He'd brush and braid our hair. It was fun. But as we grew up, he started doing weird things."

"What kind of weird things?"

"He would..." she swallowed. "He would stand behind us and touch our hair. Sometimes sneak up on us while we were watching TV. There were times we would wake up in the middle of the night because we swore he was stroking our head like a cat. But when we would look, no one was there but the door would be ajar and we had started locking him out of our room when we caught him stealing hairs from our brushes. It reached the point that when I was thirteen and Neve was fifteen, we cut off our ponytails." She let out a sharp breath, almost like a stifled laugh. "Mom was so pissed." Her face instantly became serious and stern. "She left the hair on the kitchen counter and dragged us to the walk-in salon at the mall to get our haircuts fixed. When we got home, the ponytails were gone."

Donnie remembered that day. Neve had come home with a bob, her hair reaching just to her chin. Elise, however, had her hair cropped in a male-style cut. Donnie hated it. She had been so beautiful. He couldn't understand why they would do that to themselves.

"Objection, your honor. What relevance is this to the trial?" Bridget's voice brought Donnie back to the courtroom.

"I'm sure the striking physical similarity between Elise Evans and Olivia Kincaid is obvious to even you, Mrs. Tucker. I assure you, it is relevant." Martin stared at Bridget.

The judge nodded. "Overruled. Please continue Mr. Crosby."

"Did you ever find the ponytails?" Martin turned back to Elise.

She shook her head. "No."

A woman juror with bottled black hair touched her head.

"Maybe your dad threw them away?"

She shook her head again. "He was out of town. That's why we did it that day. So he couldn't yell at us." She looked at her hands in her lap. "Donnie was the only one home when we left."

"Thank you, Miss Evans. Just one more question. What color did the defendant's mom, your sister, Neve, and your mom have?'

"Aunt Susan had blonde hair. Neve, Mom, and I all have jet-black hair."

"Thank you, Miss Evans, for confirming that the defendant has a history of stalking behavior with women with black hair."

Bridget stood and approached Elise. "Did your cousin, Donald Evans, ever cause you physical or bodily harm?"

"No."

"Never hit, kicked, or physically assaulted you or your sister?"

"No."

"Did he ever attempt to molest you?"

"No."

"Did he ever threaten to hurt or even kill you?"

"No."

"So, do you consider my client to be a violent person, in your experience?"

Elise was clearly fighting back tears. "No."

Donnie didn't like to see Elise crying. She had been like a sister to him. He watched her get up and exit the room, still refusing to make eye contact with him. It had been nearly a decade and a half since they'd spoken. There was so much he'd liked to have said to her. Did she have her own family now? Did she get her nursing degree? He was brought out of his reverie when he heard the words 'closing statements.'

Martin Crosby stood. He tugged on the bottom of his suit jacket and addressed the jury. "Ladies and Gentlemen," he said. "Over the last several days you have heard testimony from forensic experts regarding hairs, with intact root bubs, belonging to Olivia Kincaid found in Donald Evans's car. Investigators testified that they found drag marks leading from Mr. Evans's house to the creek behind his property. Ms. Kincaid's neighbor saw what could be Mr. Evans's car at her house on the night she went missing. He admits he had contact with her that day and a witness saw him staring at her lustfully. This man has a life-long history of disturbing obsession with long, black hair. His biological mother was blonde but the one woman who has always been kind to him, defended him, and raised him, has long, black hair. Could this be the root of his compulsion? I don't know. But I know her daughter, his own flesh and blood, came here today because she wanted you to know, for the sake of Olivia Kincaid, what kind of man he is." He pointed, without looking at Donnie. "Donald Evans is directly responsible for the disappearance and death of Olivia. You have heard testimony from her coworkers about how much she loved the children she worked with. You have heard from her family about how close they were. She called her mother every. Single. Day. In every testimony, they all said the same thing; the only way things would change is if she died. Please, give her family and loved ones peace by convicting the man who took her away from them. Thank you."

Bridget stood, nodded to the judge, and faced the jury. "We are all here for the same reason. We all want to see justice for a sweet woman who loved children and her family. Olivia Kincaid may be dead. But there is no evidence of that and there is certainly no evidence that she died by my client's hand. There is no gun or even blood. Investigators checked my client's house from the floorboards to the fish tank. They found hairs in his car that could have easily transferred when he bumped into her. They found drag marks leading to the water from a canoe that my client has dragged through that property for years. That's it. That's all they found. Olivia Kincaid's neighbor saw *a* Prius drive down her street but Mr. Evans's neighbor's camera proved it didn't leave his driveway that night. A man with a history of violence towards my client claims he was staring at her but, by his own admission, states Mr. Evans didn't follow her because he left the parking lot first. His cousin claims he was obsessed with her hair when they were children but that was almost 20 years ago. She admits he was never violent towards her. Donald Evans is a botanist without so much as a speeding ticket on his record. To convict him of Olivia Kincaid's murder will not be justice for her. It will allow whoever is truly responsible for her disappearance to walk free of fear of being caught. I am asking you to seek justice for Olivia by refusing to convict the wrong man so the right one can be caught."

Donnie tried to read the jury but the women were stone and emotionless. Two of the men shook their heads but Donnie was unsure if it was a good thing. He watched them file out of rows as he was handcuffed. He was led to a holding cell where he waited for hours. From there he was transported back to the jail, changed back into his jumpsuit, and given dinner. But he couldn't eat.

The next day Bridget came to visit. She assured him that a long deliberation was a good thing. But Donnie was sure she was just trying to make him feel better.

He paced in his cell the next day, and the next day, and the next. For six days he could barely eat or sleep. His freedom, maybe even his life, was in the hands of twelve strangers who had to decide if he was some kind of monster. On the seventh day, he was given his suit back and transported back to the courtroom.

As he sat and awaited his fate. His stomach had become a stone in the pit of his abdomen. His lungs refused to inflate. His jaw hurt from locking it. He looked over at Martin who was busy looking over some papers in front of him, seemingly completely disinterested in what was happening around him.

"We told the truth," Bridget tried to sound reassuring. "It'll be okay."

Donnie tried to smile but his face wouldn't work. Bridget was a lawyer so he doubted she really knew or cared about the truth, but he appreciated her efforts to ease his mind.

"All rise."

Donnie felt faint. The room was fuzzy and refusing to stay in focus. He saw twelve multi-colored blobs file into the jury box. He saw a big black blob look at something and hand it back to the first blob. The floor started moving. The walls started to distort as if made of pixels that were fragmenting.

"Not guilty."

There was a wail somewhere in the distance. Donnie didn't know if it came from him or someone behind him. His knees gave out and Bridget had to help him back into his seat.

Three days later, Donald Evans stood in his living room for the first time in nearly two years. His fish tank was bone dry. There was crusty residue from what he assumed was algae that had desiccated. A thick layer of dust covered nearly every surface. His potted plants were all long dead, brittle, and crumbling. But he was home.

He walked up to what had once been a beautiful white orchid. There were hardly any remains of the plant left. He thought about Elise and Neve. His two beautiful cousins who looked so much like their mother. He pulled the remains of the orchid out of the pot. Under the cup-shaped soil was a plastic bag. Coiled inside were two, very old, slightly dulled black ponytails. He took them out of the bag and caressed them gently. Still silky. He placed them carefully back into their resting place.

He walked over to the remains of a pygmy rose. He gently lifted it and, under the soil, was a plastic bag containing a very long, coiled, black braid. He intertwined the braid with his fingers. It still contained what had once been a bright, red bloom.

What had Bridget said? We had told the truth. Donnie had told the truth. He had bumped into Olivia that day. He had been following the flow of foot traffic and it had allowed him to watch her without drawing too much attention. He had left the parking lot first but, when he had seen her drive passed him as he was pulling out of a drive-thru two blocks away, he couldn't stop himself from following her. He saw the driveway she pulled into and the little pink house but kept driving straight, eventually going home.

He hadn't been able to stop thinking about her. He saw the shimmer of her hair in the light. He saw the way it flowed when she moved. When he had seen her let it down and it fell like a pitch waterfall, it made his heart beat faster. He had to see it again.

He had gone out the back door and retrieved his bicycle from the shed. He rode for more than thirty minutes to her house, the reward at the end keeping his legs moving.

She was asleep in her bed when he arrived. It was well past dark and he could see her by the light of the moon. Her hair glimmered like water. She had left the window open, allowing him to steal in quietly. He only meant to take some of her hair. Just a token to remember her by. But she had woken up and started to scream. On instinct, he put a hand over her nose and mouth and pinned her to the bed with his body. She fought for what felt like hours but was only a minute and a half. He hadn't meant to kill her, but no one could know he had been there. He carefully cut off the entire braid, rather than the small part he had come for, and stuffed it in his pocket.

The next night he returned and, careful that no one was watching, stuffed her in the back seat of his car. That nosey neighbor mixing up the days she had seen his car had been sheer, dumb luck. He took her home, put her in his canoe, and took her out to Little Miami River where the water was deeper and sunk her body with cinderblocks.

He looked around at the dozens of other long-dead plants. They would all need replacing. Old secrets still needed to be hidden. Donnie had told the truth. And, as they say, the truth will set you free.

Chapter 10

Grace

She is beauty. She is Elegance. Long, slender legs hitch high to an hourglass body. Such perfection knows no name, though I call her Grace. The nomer hardly seems befitting though her movements demonstrate nothing less. As if a dancer suspended in air with no sense of gravity, she moves with elegant freedom.

She is shy, more timid with guests in our home. She is a true companion waiting solemnly for my arrival each day. Night after night she learns of my lamentations, patiently listening. She has heard all of my secrets, though I know none of hers. She has seen my bare flesh and passed no judgment.

She has spun such an intricate web through my home and my life that it seems difficult to imagine it without her. But I know she is not long meant to be in this world. One day I shall look upon her corner and she will no longer be there. Her favorite resting space will be empty though her spirit will remain. The thought makes me hollow.

Though I know she is but a simple house spider, she is cherished.

Chapter 11

Eclipse 2024 Poem A

Anticipation.
　　Exhilaration.
Excitement
in the air.
An event so big
people will gather
and come from
everywhere.
Communities join
to view the specter
while faithful
will despair.
A solar event
for all man to see.
An eclipse
without compare.

Chapter 12

Jailbird

A drop of rain
upon my head.
On the day
I am to wed.
My love does smile.
My heart does sink.
My mind clouds.
It's hard to think.
A future, bright.
The unknown, grim.
Forever
I'm bound to him.
Drop. Drop. The rain
falls from the sky.
Heaven weeps.
I'll never fly.
Like a clipped bird
trapped on the ground,
in a cage
screams without sound.
My prison made.
The lock is tight.
It fits on

my finger right.
He says, "I do"
and I do too.
My fate, sealed.
Our years are few.

Chapter 13

The Flight Home

'Away' is such a unicorn of a concept. I fled to the other side of the world in search of such a thing. But life, work, everything I have left behind lurked in the shadows. I heard a phone that sounds like mine. I saw a coworker on a street corner. I had to remind myself not to look at my email with my morning coffee. I had left these things half a world a way in hope of escape before they consume me, but I fear it is too late.

    I have allowed the life I built, that I once loved, to spoil. What was once sweet is now bitter. What once filled me with pride now provides nothing but dread. Brick by brick I built a prison with blueprints for a castle. Now, I sit forty-thousand feet in the air, returning to my cell. I can hear the shackles jangling at the end. For four glorious days I glimpsed freedom, but now they wait for me, my jailors who hid in the shadows. They wait to lock me back in my keep. My unicorn remaining just out of reach.

Chapter 14

No One

No one at home.
No one to care.
No one to notice
if I'm not there.
No husband to hug
my sad away
or to tell me
It'll be okay.
My friends have gone
to live their lives.
Like ghosts in dark
we can't revive.
My job is hollow.
I know my peers.
Hardly social
all these years.
My life is quiet.
No children, so small.
No one to miss me.
No one at all.

Chapter 15

When You Want It Done

When you want it done
    Do it yourself.
Don't sit idle
like a box on a shelf.
No one will clean and
no one will cook.
To learn something new
you must open the book.
Dishes to load
 and laundry to dry.
Must weed the garden
before the vegetables die.
Garbage to toss
and floors to sweep.
A bed to be made
for somewhere clean to sleep.
To get it all done
you must do it alone.
This is YOUR castle.
This is YOUR home.

Chapter 16

Death of innocence

Sweet caress
of somber night
darkness comes
as eagle flight.
Touch of fingers,
soft with love,
warmth of heart,
pure like doves.
Be calm, breast!
Heartbeat still
of girlish laugh
and impish will.
My breath hold!
Betray me not!
This night has come
and his will wrought!
Lavish glee
his touch brings!
My virtue broken
without a ring.
But the night
Such truth hold.
No one will know.

No whispers are told.

Chapter 17

Listen up, Men

I am the voice
　of my sisters and kin.
We will fight the fight
and we will win.
Men, listen now.
I won't say it again.
You now have a choice:
Sinner or Friend?
We're all fed up
with your anger and clout.
Our minds are made up.
Don't have a doubt.
So take heed, men.
We are done with your shit.
Sit and be quiet.
We will not quit.
No touching us.
No catcalls on the street.
You are not smarter.
We're no longer meek.

Chapter 18

The Fight

It was a good day
   but now it's gone.
We were happy
but your temper has won.
It is all my fault.
That is YOUR claim.
Said something wrong
and triggered you again.
I do not know how
or why or when
you choose anger
but you'll do it again.
You say I'm silly,
making it up,
over react,
and my mood is corrupt.
But we were smiling
and then you yelled.
Got mad at me
and the scene quickly fell.
Why must we do this?
Again. Again.
You keep pushing.

This time, I will not bend.
I am over it.
And over you.
Just go ahead,
get mad. I'm angry too.

Chapter 19

Questioning Love

Tell me you love me.
　　Now say it again.
Sound like you mean it
now as you did then.
I need to hear words
you once spoke so oft
on sleepy weekends
with my heart aloft.
So lost in your words
I would find myself.
Your lips spoke so soft
to me, no one else.
I never doubt us
but I do doubt truth.
I no longer hear
it spoken by you.
So tell me, My Love,
do you have a doubt?
Do you still want me
or do you want out?

Chapter 20

My Knight Var. 2

He was my one, my knight in shining armor. He came to my rescue, riding atop his beautiful black stallion. He fought off a hundred men for me, striking down each one with a harder blow. He spoke sweet things to me that turned my cheeks the color of fresh roses. He brought me the most beautiful flowers and would only allow the daintiest and most delicious morsels to grace my tongue.

He had asked for my hand once before, and I had refused. On his second request, I could not bear to deny him. The thought that he may find another to whom he may direct his affection destroyed me. So, I agreed to be his permanent companion. He had invited me to many places and I must admit, I enjoyed his company. His wit entertained me, his mind intrigued me, and his eyes captivated me. I could not bear to be from him.

In the beginning, all was well. He continued to write me poetry and loved to be in my presence. He gave me gifts that I could hold and ones that could only touch my heart. His embrace was so full of warmth that I shuddered with chill when I could not feel it. His strong arms would wind around me and pull me close. Never would I feel any safer.

But soon, it all stopped. He would not speak his sweet poetry nor hypnotize me with his deep thoughts. I did not mind the end of the material gifts, though I hated not listening to him speak to me. Eventually, he would not look me in the eye anymore. What few times he did hold me then felt empty and hollow. Rather than feeling safe in his arms, I felt more fear than ever before. There was no trace of the love that had once been there.

I think it was my fault. Maybe I was not showing him the love he needed and greatly deserved. Maybe I was not supportive enough of him. Maybe the love that had once been had only existed in my mind. His eyes, once so full of tenderness, are now dark and hostile. His soft words have become piercing needles that prick me and cause me pain. What had I done? What pain had I caused him to force his retaliation against me. Was I not demure enough? Was I no longer beautiful enough?

Whatever caused his love to end, I now must rectify the problem. I walk around my chamber, lighting the candles, shedding light on the warm red blankets upon the bed, the heavy drapes over the windows and the bare stones that make up the walls. I pull the beautiful dagger he had given me as a gift from my pillow.

This beautiful blade which he had given me with such affection would now bring an end to the hatred he apparently bears me. I caress its fine edge with remembrance of the loving look on his face when he had presented it to me. He told me it was to ward off any other men who may try to steal him from me for if I did not cut them down, he surely would. And I had believed him then. Not anymore.

I walk to my jewelry box and remove the gold necklace he had given me when he had returned from his ventures abroad. He was so happy that I was pleased when he gave it to me. He had gently kissed my cheek and told me he had hoped it would make me happy. He said it was a simple ornament for I was more beautiful than any gem or gold.

I put the necklace on carefully and stand admiring it for a moment. I hold up the dagger again but let it drop when I look around the room and think of all the memories.

The first time I had ever told him that I loved him was in this room. We had often laid in that same bed that I stand staring at. His passion was relentless and we would often collapse into each other's arms from the exhaustion of it. As we would lie there, I would listen to him contemplate the world and its workings. He never accepted anything and questioned everything. I think that's one of the main reasons I loved him so... why I still love him.

I think though, that these memories are old. Years and years have passed since the happiness of these things. I have no recent recollections or items to look upon with such affection. Why does he suddenly loathe me so? Did I not lavish him with enough love and support? I do not know. I only know that a life without the warmth of his gaze is no life at all.

I now lay on the very same bed that we had so many times before. I hold the dagger above me. I close my eyes and see his face one last time before the blade passes through my rib cage and into the very part of me that my knight has broken.

The pain is great but not nearly as great as the pain I feel when I think that I have upset my dearest knight. As my vision blurs, I can see the already crimson bed dressings stain deeper with my blood. It is becoming more difficult for me to breathe now, but the pain is no longer there.

I see him!! My great knight!! He comes near. He looks down upon my motionless body. He gently lays a rose next to my face. I look up at him, but he turns his back on me.

    I call a whisper to him. "I lo..."

Chapter 21

The Light

When I was seven, my mother, my father, and I were sitting on the patio watching the sunset over the pond in my backyard. In the fading light, we could hear crickets chirping and bullfrogs saying good night, though we could see not a creature other than each other. Pinks and yellows with a fringe of purple draped the sky. A sweeter moment was never felt as I sat there in Daddy's lap, wrapped in his arms as we swayed in porch swing.

This serenity was not to last. I still remember exactly how it felt the first time. My head started to ache and the whites of my eyes felt as if they were burning. What was happening? I had never felt anything like this before. It was agonizing and brutal. I wanted it to end. I suddenly saw a bright flash of orange light. Everything else in the world was gone; only the light and pain existed. Was I blind? I think I was screaming but I couldn't hear anything. I couldn't feel my breath or heartbeat or my father's arms.

As suddenly as it came, the bright light and piercing pain stopped. I was on the ground, kneeling, and crying over Daddy's body. I don't remember moving. I didn't see him fall. I had no idea what was going on. My mother was on the phone with the paramedics and I desperately tried to listen and make sense of it all.

"Collapsed...No, no history...Not that I know of..." Snippets of her end of the call were all I could hear.

Hour-like moments passed and I could see the flashing lights of an ambulance pulling into my driveway. I heard one of the paramedics swear under his breath. My father was loaded onto a gurney and shoved into the back of the truck. My mother grabbed my arm and threw me into the car. We weaved and careened through traffic, narrowly evading other vehicles on the highway.

I was silent but my mother kept repeating, "Oh my God. Oh my God." These personal prayers did not seem to be helping to relax her and I was sure they were not helping Daddy. Still, I sat in silence in my seat and thought a few prayers of my own.

We arrived at the hospital shortly before the ambulance. My mother called my older brother from the hospital phone and he brought my younger brother to meet us there.

Hospital waiting areas are probably the most uncomfortable place you can think of. The walls and floors are all white. Furniture and decorations are washed out in muted blues, beige, and pink. They're meant to be calming colors. Swirling abstract art reminiscent of calm landscapes and ocean views are further meant to instill a sense of peace. But there is no peace when you are torn from a loved and forced to sit still and wait. Another young girl around my age was there with her father. We looked at each other in silent understanding.

My mother, brothers, and I all sat in that uncomfortable space. The white walls and white floors made me think of a vision of Heaven. Was that where my Father had gone? It was almost too unnerving for a seven-year-old to bear. An angel in a white lab coat came and told us that my father had had a heart attack but we could see him.

When we found Daddy, he was lying unconscious in the hospital bed. Tubes and wires connected him to all sorts of screens and dials and fluids. I watched from the doorway for hours. He never moved. His pale face and lifeless manner made him a ghost of the man I knew.

I kept thinking to myself, "This is not Daddy. Daddy can't be hurt. Nothing could ever happen to him. This isn't Daddy."

Beside him sat his ever-faithful wife. She looked up at my brothers and me. Her green eyes were bloodshot and tear stained. She squeezed the hand of her beloved one more time as she stood. She stepped as if the earth was shaking. We left feeling heartsick.

When we got outside, my oldest brother slammed his fist against the wall as hard as he could. A piece of red brick fell to the cold pavement. My younger brother and I both jumped.

"Austin!" My mother scolded him but he ignored her.

"It's not your fault," I said.

"I don't care! We could lose him! You're too young to understand, Brooke!" He shouted at me.

"We won't," I said more softly.

"How do you know?"

"I just do. Daddy can't die."

He took a deep breath. "I sure hope you're right."

He put his arm around me and we walked towards his car. His muscular sixteen-year-old arm was a comfort to me.

The next day, school went slower than ever. I swore the big clock over the doorway in the classroom was ticking in reverse at times. Every time I tried to pay attention to the class, my mind kept going back to the weakened man in the hospital bed. When at last school was dismissed, we went straight to the hospital.

A nurse was taking some of my father's blood. She smiled at us. "He's very weak. Don't stay long, he needs his rest."

Austin and I stood in the doorway after the nurse had left. I nudged him with my elbow. He slowly approached our sickly father. I stayed where I was and watched.

My brother looked back at me for some form of support. I could only look back. I didn't know what to do or what to say. I was Daddy's Little Princess. I had never had to be the strength in the family before. He gently took our father's hand and sat down in the chair beside the bed. I marveled as I witnessed something I had never seen before. My brother put his father's hand to his forehead... and cried. Large glassy tears rolled down his raw cheeks as he sobbed loudly. To this day I'm not certain if they were tears of joy because Daddy was going to be all right or tears of sadness because of the whole experience.

I walked up behind him. I put my hand on his shoulder. He leaned his head on it. I wrapped my arms around him. He embraced me back and wept into my shoulder. I buried my face in his neck and cried too. We left the hospital arm in arm.

As the days rolled by, we visited Daddy every day we could. We brought him flowers and snuck him ice cream. We were so happy when one day in September we learned he could finally come home. My brothers cleaned the whole house from top to bottom and, with a little help, I made and decorated a cake.

Unfortunately, all good things come at a price. On the night our father was supposed to come back, something very tragic happened. I felt a pain at the base of my brain once again. I could feel it creep up into my eyeballs. The orange light blared before me yet again. There was so much pain and I couldn't orient myself. When I awoke, the ivory phone in the kitchen was ringing. My brother answered the phone with a smile that quickly faded to a look of terror. Daddy's sister was driving him home from the hospital. A drunk driver had hit their car. They didn't survive.

No child should have to attend their father's funeral. That is something we are supposed to do as adults when we can mentally and emotionally cope. Yet, I stood in line between my two brothers as a man in uniform handed my weeping mother a folded-up flag. By that point, I had run out of tears. I just stood with each of my brothers holding one of my hands and prayed.

Weeks later, I tried to explain the orange flash to my mother. Fearing something genetic that could have caused both the orange light and Daddy's heart disease, she took me to the doctor the following week. He said from what I had described, it sounded like I had had a seizure. There are types that would not cause my body to convulse violently like what happens when most people think a seizure should look like. He said that since I had no history or evidence of a seizure, it was probably the subconscious mind of a young girl trying to distract herself from the horrifying truth of her dying father. I tried to explain that it had happened BEFORE Daddy's heart attack, but my words fell on deaf ears. He prescribed some medication and we left the office

I confided in my best friend, Melissa, as most little girls do. She said her Momma liked to call in to talk to a psychic who could tell her the future and maybe I was psychic. Maybe I couldn't see the future but the ghosts were warning me like the Jamaican lady on TV. It sounded a little crazy but it was the best theory we had.

We assumed the medication had worked since I did not see any more orange flashes for years. Life had moved on. Austin had moved out and it was up to my little brother and I to tend to our still heartbroken mother. She never fully recovered from Daddy's death and so we took up the mantle of keeping things tidy and tracking the schedules. It was hard for two little kids, but she needed us.

Then, when I was thirteen, I was riding in the car with Austin when he had picked me up from soccer practice. It was a bright summer day in the mid-afternoon. There were neither clouds in the sky nor cares in the world. My brother's pitiful little Ford puttered along and jerked a little every few moments. We were talking and laughing about the man who stood watering his yard while wearing a raincoat. It was a perfect moment. But only a moment. I felt a familiar pain in the back of my head again. "Oh no," I thought. Before I could tell My brother to stop the car, that horrible color blared before me.

My neck throbbed and my leg was seeping blood. There was a tree where the driver's seat should have been and my brother was pushed up against me. I looked him over, praying he was still alive. His head was bloody and he looked drugged as his head flopped over to look back at me.

"Get out of the car." He gulped harshly.

I climbed out through the passenger side window. "Austin?"

"Get help," he breathed heavily. "I'm trapped."

I ran to the road and began to scream and wave my arms. "Somebody! Please help!"

If only we had had cell phones back then, maybe things would have ended differently. I heard a funny WHOOSH noise and turned my head back to the car. Fire. I ran back to the car and tried frantically to pull my brother to safety.

"Get back, Brooke! Go get help!" His final words.

I was crying and screaming and the flames moved from the hood into the cab of the car. He was screaming in pain, I knew he was, but I couldn't hear him. Dancing shades of yellow and orange engulfed the car and my brother and instantaneously raced up the tree. There was not enough of his corpse left for a proper burial.

    I don't know who had called for help, but they were too late. The paramedics patched me up and sent me to the hospital. I told my tending doctor at the emergency room about the orange flash I had seen just prior to the crash and about my previous experience with the phenomena. He ran a few tests, prescribed some new drugs, and whispered to my mother that he recommend I see a therapist.

The police said the old clunker car had jerked and when my brother tried to correct it, he turned too hard and threw the car into the tree. Cars don't mysteriously jerk and I tried to argue that point, but what does a teenage girl know?

It was decided that we could not afford a therapist and the new drugs seemed to be working. Again, I went a few years without the flash of light. I thought I was cured. Alas, I was wrong again. I was sixteen. It was very late one Saturday night. A sudden, uneasy feeling awakened me. I felt a pain force its way into the back of my eyes.

"Oh no," I thought. "Not again."

Once again, the phone rang. I pulled the receiver off the soccer ball shaped phone next to my bed.

"Brooke?" An out-of-breath and terrified voice came from the other end.

"Yeah?"

"It's Melissa. I need your help. A bunch of girls are chasing me. Trying to get my new shoes. You have to come get me. They're going to kill me."

I bolted straight up in bed. "Where are you? I'm coming right now." I started to pull on my shoes.

"I'm at the phone booth at the corner Smith and Riley."

"Hey!" I heard a new voice shout. "I thought we told you to give up those shoes!" There was silence. "You callin' the cops?"

"No. No, not at all," Melissa's voice was full of terror.

"I'll bet. You try to turn us in and you got to pay."

"I didn't try to turn you in."

"Right." I heard a gasp and two gunshots. Melissa let out the most dreadful scream of pain and fear that has ever broken the air.

"Melissa?! Melissa!!" I screamed into the phone. I slammed down the receiver and dialed 911.

"911 emergency," the operator answered.

"My friend has just been shot." I spoke hurriedly and fearfully.

"Where are you?"

"I'm at home. She called me just before she was shot."

"Do you know where she is?"

"The phone booth on the corner of Smith and Riley."

"What is your address?" I gave her the information. "Don't worry. I've sent an ambulance to her. Stay right where you are."

"Thank you." I hung up the phone and sat on my bed. What was happening to me? What was happening to the people I loved?

In a few minutes, the police came banging on the door. They asked me some questions while my mother attempted to comfort me. I told them the answers to the best to my knowledge.

A young officer came in from the squad car and told me that they had found Melissa and she was at Faithful Hospital.

In the company of Melissa's parents, we waited anxiously in the waiting room. I know it had been years ago, but that same uneasy feeling that had crept over me when I sat in the very same chair the night my father had had his heart attack once again filled my heart. It felt as if it was going to choke the very life out of breast.

Melissa's dad paced nervously and kept slamming his large fist into the open palm of his other hand. I sat in my chair staring straight ahead in shock. I kept running the image of her being hit by the bullets and her body falling to the cold pavement in my head. I couldn't get the sound of her scream out of my mind.

The doctor finally came down the hallway. She looked rigid and took her steps carefully. "She lost and awful lot of blood..."

This time, there was no debate. My mother pulled together some money and a week later, I was in almost daily therapy sessions and on a slew of new medications. Red, blue, yellow, and white tablets waited for me twice a day. They felt like eyes staring at me through the amber plastic vials. They were just sitting there and waiting to enter my system and impinge on my body in ways I could not and dared not know.

This time I was so sure I was cured. I was wrong again. Five years without an 'episode' as my therapist called them. Five years of calming harmony and relaxation. Only five years. I was twenty-one. My mother didn't believe in the orange light. She believed it was whatever the therapist told her; a seizure or an 'episode.' Whatever they had been were nonexistent. I continued to see my therapist almost weekly simply to appease my mother.

One day, I was sitting on my porch steps waiting for my younger to come home from school. The orange suddenly flashed more brilliantly than ever before. I fell backwards and hit my head on the concrete stairs.

I had a dream about a little boy on the corner where my brother's bus would let him off. There was a man slowly walking up behind him. I didn't know either of them, but I knew in the pit of my stomach that something was very wrong. That little boy was not safe.

I had not been that scared since that night my friend could not answer my screams. What was I going to do? I looked over and saw my mother's garden trowel sticking in the dirt. I grabbed it and ran towards the ghostly man. I wasn't going to let this strange boy die like my father and brother and friend. I couldn't.

I ran up to the man who was now coming towards me. I grabbed his arm and spun him around. I threw him on the ground and rammed the small shovel into his spine. I rolled him over and again jammed the point into his body, this time piercing his heart. It was such a vivid dream. I even remember the warmth of the blood on my hands.

When I woke up, I was in the hospital. My mother was sitting nearby. She was shaking and crying. Her skin was colorless and sick-looking. I found out from a nurse that there was no strange man or boy on the corner but what I had done had not been a dream either. It was my brother walking home from school. I had killed him with a garden trowel. I had killed my last sibling.

Seizure. Episode. Precognition. Schizophrenia. Does it even matter anymore? Will I ever forgive myself? Can my mother ever forgive me?

Chapter 22

December 3rd

My heart does hurt.
It's plain to see.
What the Hell
is wrong with me?
My love is strong.
You claim it's weak.
I can't fill
the thing you seek.
I try and try.
It's not enough.
Loving you
shouldn't be tough.
Please don't leave me
broken hearted.
My deep love's
not departed.
I fight for us.
Will you the same?
Now this strife
has to be tamed.

Chapter 23

Alive

Everything is okay.
Everything is fine.
Nothing's putting pressure
on this broken heart of mine

No one here is yelling.
Every face, a smile.
If I keep doing this
maybe it will stick a while.

My head is not throbbing.
My stomach does not churn.
Physically, I'm as fit
as a wood pile that burns.

More work, more work, more work.
Never get to play.
Every night may be dark,
but so is every day.

So I keep on pushing.
Fighting to survive.

Wishing that someday I
might finally feel alive.

Chapter 24

Belgium and Blood

His breath is cold on my back. I remember how warm it used to be. A feeling like a tiny autumn breeze kisses my spine between my shoulder blades. A soft, droning snore accompanies the rhythmic movement of his chest. He holds me close, arms wrapped around my abdomen as if afraid to let me go. I revel in this. Everything about what we are doing is wrong. I know this but I cannot deny him. It would be like trying to deny myself oxygen to breathe.

He has been the one thing that keeps my heart beating for nearly half a decade. He was – is – a kind soul. He loves cats, he supports my career, and has never raised his voice to me. I helped tutor him through university, nursed him through depression when his mother passed away, and introduced him to sushi. He tolerates my anxiety and I tolerate his terrible cooking. Every day I come home to him and the weight of existence is lifted as he wraps me in his arms. We are two halves that make each other whole.

The changes, subtle at first, began a few weeks ago. He had been requested on a business trip to Belgium to inspect a very expensive piece of equipment his company was purchasing. He asked if I had wanted to join him so that we could stay a few extra days and have some time to ourselves but I declined. My students had finals approaching and they needed me if they were to succeed. So, he went alone. Every day my phone would ding with pictures of delicious looking foods and glasses of wine. Most of it didn't look like things he would normally eat but, when in Belgium... He even sent pictures of Antwerp's hands he saw in a store, which I found disgusting and vulgar. Brussels is six hours ahead of Cincinnati and he was careful not to call when I would be sleeping. However, every morning at 6am, I would get a text message to tell me he loved me and to have a good day. At my lunch time, he would be winding down his day before bed and would always call to tell me how much he missed me. It sounds mawkish, but I missed him too and especially at night. There was no one at home to hug the day's stress away. Dinner for two was for just me and the cat who wasn't much of a conversationalist. The bed felt like an immense and barren flatland without his weight. His arms weren't there to make me feel safe and warm. The bedroom seemed as quiet as a tomb without his snores to lull me to sleep. Suffice it to say, I wanted him home and with me.

My wish finally came true after sixteen days of aching. I sat on the couch, listening to music and reading the latest hardback novel I'd picked up at the library when I saw his car pull into the drive. When he came in through the kitchen door, I threw my arms around him. He dropped his bag (very nearly on the cat at our feet) and embraced me back. We kissed, but it lacked the passion he usually expressed. I became aware that he felt thinner, bonier. I pulled back and held his face in my hands while I gazed into his eyes. His once vibrant blues we set back in the sockets and dulled. His skin seemed pale and cold to the touch. I expressed my concern, but he assured me it was just exhaustion from the flight. We shared a plate of cheese and crackers and glasses of wine while he showed me pictures on his phone. I asked him about a wound on his wrist and he said he had slammed it in a door. He had never lied to me before. I noticed he hadn't eaten much and his voice seemed low and slow. I recommended we go to bed so he could rest and he seemed relieved as he agreed.

But this was only the beginning of his bizarre behavior. He seemed more sullen and surly. He used to become petulant when he was hungry and this seemed very similar. The man once would cook a beautiful steak into something of similar texture to the sole of a shoe. After he returned from Belgium, he preferred his meat just warmed and would devour most supper as if it were his last meal. Kisses were reduced to simple pecks on the cheek or lips. He was once very dutiful about making sure we both went to bed at 930pm and he woke readily at 5am, often without an alarm clock. But instead, he now struggled to fall asleep at night and wake up in the morning. For the first week, I was convinced it was due to the change in time between Europe and home, but he only seemed to be getting worse instead of better. His skin lost its healthy glow and dark circles deepened under his eyes. His touch was constantly cold and clammy. When we lay in bed at night, he would try to hold me but he felt like a stranger. Eventually, he would toss and turn, unable to sleep, and inevitably go to his office to work. I insisted he see a doctor but he assured me he would be fine. He worsened. Day after day I watched him deteriorate. He tried to be himself. He tried to play games with me and show interest in my lesson plans, but I could see that his heart wasn't in it.

I missed him. I missed his sense of humor. I missed his strength. I missed his tenderness and when he would gently make love to me. I missed the expressiveness of his eyes and the soft feel of his lips against mine. He wasn't my Love anymore. He was an intruder into our lives. Attempts to talk to him were met with anger or sadness but no resolutions.

One day he came home from work, looking more like an animated corpse than ever, but with a smile on his face. He said the extra work he had done instead of sleeping had earned him a bonus at work. I hugged him and kissed him. He kissed me back. And the kiss deepened. And he pulled me close. He felt more like the man I fell in love with than he had in weeks. I pressed my body against him, wanting to pull him inside me. I felt his teeth graze my lower lip and he released me. I felt excitement as I led him back to the bedroom. He seemed apprehensive but, as I stood before him, my flesh exposed and waiting, I saw pure desire in his eyes. He pushed me onto the bed and climbed on top of me, running his hands and lips all over my skin. He had never been so aggressive and forceful when making love to me before. I found it exhilarating. As I sat on his lap, our bodies pressed together with his face in my neck, I felt a tiny stab of pain in my shoulder, and a few seconds later, I was on the floor.

He stood in the corner with a look of horror on his face. His face? The face that showed on the man I loved was not his own. This face seemed longer and the eyes seemed darker. But as he stood panting, eyes wide at what he had just done, I could see bulges just above the tips of his canine teeth that were protruding from behind his lips. I touched my shoulder. It was warm, wet, and sticky. I brought my hand back and looked at my blood. He crumpled to the floor, holding his head in his hands and apologizing.

I didn't blink as I looked from him to my bloody fingers and back again. This wasn't real. Vampires lived in Transylvania, not Belgium. What was I saying? Vampires didn't EXIST. But there he was, pale and thin, craving raw red meat... retractable fangs peeking from his mouth. It all made sense but it made no sense at all.

I knelt in front of him. He sobbed, begged forgiveness, and refused to look at me. I don't know what made me do it. Maybe sympathy or empathy or the pain of seeing my beloved in such a state. I took his head in my hands and lifted it until his eyes met mine. He kept telling me 'no' but I used my bloody index finger to shush him.

"Drink me," I whispered.

His eyes doubled in size and he shook his head violently in refusal. I then slipped my bloody finger into his mouth and he froze. I could see the yearning, the starvation, and the desperation in those blues.

"It'll be okay," I assured him.

I could see his will power snap like a twig that was trod upon. He lifted me back into the bed and he pressed his lips to my shoulder. The intimacy of that night was the type that belonged in erotic novels. I gave my body and blood to him freely and was rewarded with electrifying sensations.

The next morning, I woke to the sound of butter in the skillet and the heavenly smells of bacon and coffee. I stumbled into the kitchen and he helped me into a chair at the table. He set a mug of coffee and a plate of bacon and eggs in front of me, telling me I needed to eat well to replace what he took.

"Tell me everything," I said as I shoveled scrambled eggs into my maw.

I couldn't help but notice how virile he looked. His skin was a healthy tan color and he seemed less bony. The dark rings under his eyes had vanished and those beautiful blues had their sparkle again. I analyzed his appearance and listened as he explained that on his second night in Belgium, he had gone out for drinks with the representatives from the factory. The next morning, he woke up in his hotel feeling dizzy and weak with two puncture marks on his wrist. He handed me a note that had been left on the bedside table. In broken English, it explained that his attacker had slipped a drug in his drink. He had been taken back to his hotel where the unknown person fed on his wrist. It explained that they had accidentally bitten hard enough to inject venom into the wound and he would turn into one of them.

"Venom?" I asked.

He indicated the bulges that I had seen above his teeth and I nodded.

The letter went on to explain that he would need to feed once a month to survive and as long as he didn't use his venom (with no instructions as to how to control this) his victims would not turn. The attacker apologized for what he or she had done and assured him it was an accident because they were just so hungry. That was it. He was a victim simply because he was easy prey. His life was forever changed not because he was special, but because he was simple.

I looked up at my Love and he stared at the mug of coffee in front of him. Without looking at me, he explained that he thought it was a hoax until he realized that he was hungry but food just wasn't filling and then the insomnia started. He thought about taking the note to the police, but they would just take him for a mad man. In his down time from the factory, he tried to get camera footage from the bar or the hotel, but there was nothing to see on the recordings. He began visiting occult shops and asking questions about local vampire lore. One shop he was fairly certain was run by another vampire who was able to explain the venom sacks, even though they were not part of lore. As far as he understood, he would live a normal life span though hardly ever get sick. Anything that could kill a man could kill him. He was still himself but would need a blood meal at least once a month to survive. He took a deep breath and told me he kept sending me pictures and calling because he didn't want to worry me. But when he came home and held me, he knew he could never live with himself if he ever hurt me but also that he would rather die than live without me.

I looked down at my now-empty plate. I had not noticed how hungry I had been. We sat in a strained silence while I contemplated my bacon and eggs. I was hungry. I hadn't even known I was hungry. Yet, I could eat what I wanted and be fulfilled. My Love no longer had that choice. He would live in a constant state of hunger and could easily starve. I would not have believed any of this at all if I hadn't seen it unfold with my own eyes. I touched the puncture on my shoulder and watched him wince. He looked healthy though not at all happy. It had been my blood that made him that way. It would be my blood that would keep him that way. We argued but, in the end, I won. He would feed on me and only me.

So now we lay in bed. His arms are around me once again. His dull snoring will help me drift to sleep. He is sated for now but in a month, he will need to feed again and I will be here.

Chapter 25

August 9th

Some days are a little harder.
    Some days a little rough.
It doesn't matter what I do
it'll never be enough.
When getting up's a struggle
and eating is a chore
and when I have run out of spoons
someone will ask for more.
Sleep is but an empty dream
and my stomach acid churns
and I'll keep on fighting tears
that cause my eyes to burn.
Because I must keep fighting
and getting out of bed
and taking one day at a time
until it is the end.

Chapter 26

August 19th Poem A

What's the point in talking
    if you won't listen to me speak?
When I need you to hold me up,
instead you call me weak.
When I tell you that I'm hurting
and want to crawl away to cry
you shrug your arms and shake your head
and on insist on asking why.
When I'm open and I'm honest
about feeling overwhelmed
you bark more orders at me
and say you're taking the helm.
When I tell you I feel I'm drowning
and that my life is such a mess
you say there's something wrong with me
but what is anyone's guess.
So now I've finished talking.
I'll keep it all inside
and watch you get more angry
that in you I won't confide.
Because why should I keep talking?

My heart is wearing thin.
I've tried to speak this one last time
and you're ignoring me again.

Chapter 27

Lies you sing

Sing the song
    my heart knows so well.
Beat for beat
the lies you tell.
Lyrics ring
so loud and so bold
tell of love
when we grow old.
What a tune
you belt out so clear!
An opera
for all to hear.
'Tis a tale.
We both know it's true.
Verse for verse
pretense from you.
We won't heal
as you often claim.
If I harken,
I am insane.
So silence.
No more melody.
Hold your breath

for you and me.
Ballad done
and song is sung.
I leave you.
My heart strings strung.

Chapter 28

September 1st

It's one of those days,
　　dark as the night.
Spirit is broken.
No future bright.

No one to hear me.
Just my own thoughts.
Confusion abound.
Overwhelm wrought.

I can hear the words
spoken to me
but can't understand
what can they mean?

The harder I try
the less I know
further I fall.
I'm my own foe.

I'm ready to quit.
Just give up now.
Close the curtains,

take my last bow

I'm done with the fight.
None left to give.
Torn to pieces.
No will to live.

Chapter 29

The Pain no one Talks About

You know what no one ever talks about with depression? How much it hurts. Of course, there is focus on the emotional pain but what about the physical pain?

The tension headaches are agony. Your head is trapped in a vice. Squeezing. Putting pressure on your temples and forcing your brain into the forehead part of your skull. Or worse, there is a little gremlin inside your head chiseling away with an icepick. If you're lucky, it'll end there. But sometimes, it will become a migraine. Blinding pain is interspersed with bursts of white light every time there is a sharp noise. The low, buzzing vibrations of electricity reverberate through your core. The resulting nausea prevents you from keeping any food in your body long enough to begin digestion and you become weak and disoriented.

The stiffness in your shoulders and neck prevent any kind of comfort in a sleeping or lying position. You've carried the weight of existing all day and that crushing pressure has caused your muscles to tense for so long, they refuse to relax. The constant feeling like you are shrugging your shoulders is enough to drive a person mad. No amount of rolling your neck or stretching your back provides relief. Turning your head, reaching foreword, and bending over all become memories.

It's a coin toss to determine if the insomnia is from the muscle stiffness and inability to get comfortable or if it is the product of the restless mind. *Tomorrow, I need to go to the grocery. Saturday, I need to take the cat to the vet and shop for new shoes. Did I log out of the computer at work? If I don't make that deal my boss is going to be so pissed.* But then there are loud, rumbling snores next to you shaking the bed, further preventing rest. You spend the night tossing and turning. The tick, tick, tick, of the clock on the wall counts down the seconds until you have to roll out of bed, ignore the pain and exhaustion, and pretend that everything is okay. You may get lucky and sneak an hour or two of something that resembles rest before the inevitable cacophony of alarms signal the new day. The fatigue feeds into the headache and the nausea, so you caffeinate.

Caffeine. That magical, miracle, wonder-drug that allows you to function. It combats headaches and lethargy. Whether it's coffee, tea, soda, or an energy drink, it washes down the famotidine for the stomach and the acetaminophen for the head and the assorted other things that allow you to simulate happiness.

You put the waffles in the toaster and cut up the fruit for your partner. You try to make their day a little easier but you won't eat any of it. Eating is just one more chore.

Then off to work. As you pull into the parking lot you can feel your chest constrict. You feel your skin get hot as your heartbeat rises. You feel that inevitable anxiety that comes with knowing you are good at your job so expectations are high. It feels as though boulders are stacked on your rib cage as you fight to breathe. Every breath feels like a BB shot to the lungs as you fight to gain control of yourself... and you prevail.

You spend the day smiling. You don't want to smile. You want to fall into the floor or become one with the walls. You want to vanish. Not exist. Carpet doesn't feel pain. Drywall isn't sad. But disappearing is not an option and neither is allowing those around you to know your pain So you smile. Your cheeks hurt from it but still you persist. People on the other end of the phone can hear if you are not smiling and coworkers ask questions when you frown.

Then to home where your partner provides a hug and comfort, but the pain endures. The head, the heart, the stomach, the muscles, and the lungs all cry in anguish. There is no relief and you just want the pain to end.

Chapter 30

The Road of Marriage

Hand in hand
    we walk together.
Once a time
we said forever.
Started young
but now we are old.
Love to last
as we were told.
Arm in arm
we have trod this life.
You, husband
and me as your wife.
"Until death"
is what we had said.
Each clinging
'Til the other's dead.
Gentle touch.
We cannot let go.
When one dies
the other will follow.

Chapter 31

The Art Museum

There is magic
   within these walls.
A spell
upon the roof.
No stress or fear
haunts these halls.
The smiles
are all the proof.
I inhale deep
the scent of peace.
So calm.
I feel relief.
All my worries
of mind do cease
and hope
becomes belief.

Chapter 32

The Tracks

As inspired by the painting "Lot's Wife" by Anselm Kiefer

We walked along the empty tracks, kicking up dust and gravel and disturbing the roaches beneath. This stretch of tracks had long been abandoned, bringing about the slow, agonizing death of our little town. Once these tracks brought in workers and carried out the products our factories milled. Then, one day, the trains stopped. The people stopped coming, the flow of the steel we milled slowed to a trickle, and factories shut down one by one until only one remained working.

I could see them. Shapeless, grey cenotaphs against a low-hung sky. No sun shone here. As we walked towards the bleak horizon, the tracks intertwined and split. One set headed towards what was familiar. Those tombs we were destined to be buried in, just like our fathers. The other stretched to the unknown. All we could see was empty, slate colored sky with nothingness beneath it.

We made a choice that day and headed to the unknown. There was nothing to guide us. There was no family or familiarity but we chose to take a different track. We were terrified and held each other's hand for support. And we walked. We walked for ages with no food in our bellies or shelter when the rain fell. But we walked on, following tracks neither we nor our fathers had trod before with hope of something better.

We came across a body. It was soggy from the rain and bloated from neglect. Flies feasted on tears and the flesh as birds had already claimed the eyes. He, too, had walked away from what was known. But he had given in to despair and allowed the world to eat him alive.

Should we have done the same? We turned to look back and saw those familiar, shapeless figures. Their safety was a fate worse than death and we turned back to the blank sky. And we walked.

The tracks became more frangible. The wood, rotted and forgotten, split and disintegrated under our feet. The rails, oxidized and frail, offered no support.

But we still followed the tracks through the muck and rot and rain. Until the day the tracks were clean. The rails were strong and the wood was fresh. Bolstered, we pressed on. The sky before us was lighter now but still grey and empty. In the distance, we heard a train and smelled bread for our bellies and we knew we had followed the right track.

Chapter 33

Giver and Taker

I am the taker
   and you are the giver.
I asked for a pond
and you gave me a river.
I ask for hug
and you will say no
but if I need a vacation
you say I must go.
It's not enough
that I cook but don't serve.
Then you take me out
and I eat with verve.
I can't afford nice things
so you buy them for me.
I asked you not to.
You say it brings you glee.
You give me things
I asked you not to
and if I don't take them
a row will ensue.
So why are you mad
when I take what you give?
I don't need these things

in order to live.
I have not the funds
to spoil you back.
It is not desire
but money I lack.
I give what I can
but you always want more.
What more can I do?
I'm just too poor.
I scratch your back
and rub your feet
and try little things
your needs to meet.
If I dare say no
you'll certainly be mad.
Sometimes I'm tired
and sometimes I'm sad.
What little I do
won't ever be enough.
Things like this
are just too tough.

Chapter 34

Broken Trust

When trust is broken
It's gone for good.
You think you might
or ought or could
repair the damage
you reaped and sown.
Good intensions
you thought were shown.
But lies were spoken
and secrets kept
and deceit wrought
and still, you wept.
This is what you made.
My fault, you claimed.
You thought I'd break
and take the blame.
Instead you were caught.
You can't deny
when confronted,
the more you lied.
Such nonsense now.
Our friendship done.
Comfort yourself.

Our course is run.

Chapter 35

To Blame

Once again, you blame me
When something has gone wrong.
You raise your voice
And shake your fist,
Stay distant all day long.

It's all my fault, you say.
When I'm not at your call.
Your face is red.
Your teeth are bared.
Expecting me to fall.

But, you underestimate
The power that I have.
You close your eyes
And shake your head,
Split my heart in half.

Now tell me, dear lover,
Why am I at fault?
You gape your mouth
And sneer your lip,
Your game comes to a halt.

No more pointing fingers
When you know you're to blame
You drop your fist
And hold your tongue.
I'm not doing this again.

Chapter 36

Sticks and Stones

"Sticks and stones
And broken bones."
These words
are often said.
It's fun to laugh
at such things
until someone
ends up dead.
"Words are wind.
They cause no pain."
Such people
have insisted.
Tears are dried
and bruises healed
until noose or gun
enlisted.
Songs are sung
and prayer rehearsed
for the broken
and dead of shame.
We forget
no cowardice,
but bullies are

who to blame.

Chapter 37

The Joy of Halloween

I tried to play around with skipping rhythms but I'm not sure it worked as I intended.

    Trick or treat
    something fun or sweet
    the little ghoulies ask
    Once a year
    the children don their
    scariest cape or mask

Oh, what fun
    for on that night
    they squeal with Glee
    and utter Delight

Parents trudge
    on sleepy toes
    to the next porch
    where the pumpkin glows

Work all day
    and march all eve

the children's joy
give air to breathe

'Tis Halloween
   this night in fall
   that brings such happiness
   for adults and small

Chapter 38

Iliana the Monster

My name is Iliana and I am a monster.

I was adopted. Momma never made any secret of that. My birth mother had been a friend of hers who left me in her care and fled shortly after I was born. When I was young, I would ask about her. I was assured that I would grow up to be as smart and beautiful as her one day. When I asked why she left, I was told she had to and that was all. Eventually, I stopped asking.

Growing up, I knew I was different and not only because I was adopted. When I was little and I would play with the other kids, I felt their joy. More than that, I imbibed it. Their laughter and mirth made me happy and filled me with more energy while they seemed to tire easily and playtime was often cut short.

As I got older, I noticed the boys paid more attention to me than the other girls. Momma told me it was just because I was so pretty but I could always see the worry that touched her eyes. When I turned thirteen, I could no longer ignore the lingering, longing gazes of still older men. Even my teachers were drawn to stare at me while I worked. They'd find excuses to lay their hands on my shoulders or touch my back to guide me down the hall.

My best friend since childhood was Elisa. She was a saucy redhead with dreams of opening a bakery. She and I grew up across the street from each other. We called each other sisters, told each other secrets, and were virtually inseparable. She was not oblivious to the unusual treatment I received but she tried to be supportive. She told me not to worry and ignore them. She helped me pick out and dress in oversized hoodies, jeans, and sometimes hats that I could pull over my face. Even in the summer heat, I would be baking in my wardrobe but I didn't care. I tried to stay covered up. I tried to stay hidden. I eventually refused to answer questions in class or anything else that may draw attention to myself. It didn't matter. Eyes and heads still tuned in my direction.

Entering high school is hard for anyone but worse for me. For most girls, makeup became more glamorous, shorts got shorter, hair became more elaborate, and after classes were meant to be filled with soccer, cheerleading, or going shopping with friends. I, for the most part, traveled between home, school, and Elisa's house. My wardrobe was mostly black, hoods and hats covered my head, and makeup was an art form that I had no desire to master. Suffice it to say, I was not popular amongst the other girls and was often bullied for being different.

I was fourteen and in my freshman year when I was paired with a boy named Noah for a project in our physics class. He was tall and lean. He favored blue plaid and checker print shirts. The blue matched his eyes which were framed with wire-rimmed glasses. His hair was always short and neat. He tended to sit near the windows of the classroom and gaze out over the courtyard, lost in his own imagination. He wasn't popular in the traditional high school freshman sense, but that didn't stop the popular girls from swooning over him and vying for his attention.

The partnership gave them a new reason to dislike me.

The assignment was to make a car powered by nothing more than the potential energy stored in a rat trap. There would be a competition and the car that went the farthest won a prize.

It seemed simple enough but there were a great deal of creative differences and design concept disputes between Noah and me.

"I think we should go with a smaller axel with smaller wheels so we get a larger number of rotations of the wheels per string pull." His voice was exacerbated and bordered on unhinged.

"It won't matter if we get a larger number of rotations if the surface area of the wheel is too small," I countered, equally exhausted by the arguments.

We were on the verge of yelling loud enough to be heard the next block over. We were seated at a picnic table outside the public library as the discussion had already become too heated and we were asked to take it outside.

"You still get more rotations and therefore more distance out of a bottle cap than the lid to a pickle jar."

I fought to keep my self-control. "Then why are the tires on the back of NASCAR cars bigger than the ones in the front?"

He opened his mouth to rebut but closed it.

"Exactly!" I yelled a little too loud. "We will get the same amount of string around the axel in one pull. We may get more rotations per pull but less surface area equals less distance."

He ground his jaws. I could see the hamster running the wheel in his brain. It was spinning as fast as it could but going absolutely nowhere. I won.

"Fine," he said grudgingly. "But you'd better be right."

"Of course I'm right. I also already have an A in class. What do you have?"

His jaw set.

We met at the library once per week to discuss design ideas and eventually at his house to work on prototypes. His dad allowed us access to his tools and scrap pieces of wood. Momma was none too happy about me spending time at a boy's house and my assurances that his parents and siblings were home did little to ease her discomfort. I felt a twinge of guilt about it. The truth was, I liked spending time with Noah. He didn't stare at me like the other boys. He didn't sneak up behind me just to try to stand close to me. He didn't sniff the air in my wake like a bloodhound. He didn't do any of the things that made me feel like I needed to hide. Being with him was like being with Elisa. I was just myself, not a freak of nature or a rose on display.

Just Iliana.

Our final prototype consisted of the assigned rat trap mounted to a piece of two-by-four, a half-inch dowel for axels, some old ribbon I'd found in a craft box in Momma's closet, and eight-inch wooden wheels we had made from discs we found at a craft store.

We set it at our designated starting line (the crack in the sidewalk that aligned with his mailbox). We wound the ribbon as we pulled back on the rat trap and released it. We watched it pass his neighbor's driveway. And the next. And it kept going farther than any prototype we had made to that point. We smiled and laughed and jumped up and down with glee. He pulled me into a hug mid-jump and then... he kissed me.

I had never been kissed before but at that moment, I needed it. It was like I was drowning and his kiss was the oxygen I needed to survive. I pulled him close to me. I wanted to pull him inside of me. Every cell in my body awakened and I kissed him deeper.

I became suddenly aware that his lips were limp but his body was ridged and shaking. I released him. His eyes were rolled into his skull and he was convulsing.

I screamed.

The entire neighborhood heard me and maybe a few blocks over. I kept screaming, not knowing what had happened or what to do. His parents rushed out the front door. In a frenzied chaos that I can only partially remember, they got me and their son into the car and drove us to the hospital. I was repeatedly questioned and told them all (his parents, the nurse, and the doctor) the same thing. I kissed him and he seized.

When Momma came to pick me up, I melted into her arms and sobbed into her shoulder. She asked me what happened. I told her the same thing. I kissed him and he seized. Her expression was grim as she thanked Noah's parents for watching after me and offered her prayers for his recovery.

What followed wasn't real. It was a dream. A nightmare. I was sure of it. Everything that existed around me seemed noncorporeal. I could see it all but I couldn't feel anything I touched. I couldn't smell the city or hear Momma muttering to herself beside me as she drove. The world was made of colors and shapes that I was completely incapable of interacting with.

At home, I went directly to my bedroom and collapsed on my quilt. I was numb and exhausted but glad to be back surrounded by my own things. There is immeasurable comfort in familiarity. I don't know how or when I drifted to sleep or how long I had stayed unconscious, but I didn't stir until I heard my name being called from downstairs. A starless sky hung outside my window and I knew it was not yet morning.

As I descended the stairs, I heard hushed voices speaking frantically in the kitchen. One was Momma's but I didn't recognize the other. When I rounded the corner, the most beautiful woman I had ever seen was seated at the kitchen table with a cup of tea in her fingers. Her skin, slightly tan, was without a single freckle or blemish. Her eyes were a rich brown with flecks of green like mine and accentuated with long, perfect lashes. Her aquiline nose was seated above full, naturally pink lips and a pointed chin that reached back up to high cheekbones. All were framed by smooth, chocolate curls that extended down to her hips. She wore a white lace sundress, odd for this time of year, which showed off all of her curves. A single seashell on a simple gold chain rested at the top of her cleavage. She smiled at me, revealing teeth that may as well have been made of pearls. As soon as I looked into her eyes and saw the same eyes that had looked back at me from the mirror all my life, I knew who she was. And I was afraid.

As if sensing my alarm, she stood, her curls and flowing lace moving as if with an invisible ocean wave.

"Iliana—," she started.

My jaw dropped and my mouth gaped. My chest constricted and I felt as though I couldn't breathe. I was a fish drowning in air. A million emotions all vied for control at the sound of her voice. Confusion at her sudden appearance. Anger at her absence. Longing for her attention. Rage at her mere presence.

"You have every right to feel all of those things," she said gently.

"You're my mother," I said without breath.

Momma, who I had not noticed position herself behind me, rested her hand on my shoulder. "Yes."

"Wh-what's going on?" It appeared that confusion was the emotion that surfaced first and took control of my voice.

Momma bit her lower lip and went to stand next to my mother. "We had a discussion and decided that there are certain things we cannot keep from you anymore. You need to know who and what you are."

My eyes darted between the two women in front of me. My stomach was balling up inside me like a fist getting ready to fight.

"I think you should sit," the beautiful woman, my mother, said. "And have some tea."

Every fiber of my being told me to be wary of this woman. She radiated something I couldn't identify but I feared it. I fought to ignore the alarm bells going off inside my head as I did as I was told. I kept my eyes locked with hers and we both sat. Momma set a mug of hot water in front of me. My mother slid her mug across the table and gently touched it to mine. The water in my mug turned the same yellow-brown as the contents of hers. I felt my eyes widen.

"I hope you like chamomile with honey," she said gently.

I nodded, still examining the mug and trying to understand what had just happened.

"Drink," Momma said, taking a seat at the round table halfway between us.

I looked at the mug, to the woman, then to Momma. Momma nodded, encouragingly.

"But-," I started.

"Drink," she said more firmly.

I picked up the mug and sipped. I trusted that Momma would not allow this woman to poison me but I did feel like Snow White being encouraged to eat the apple. As the hot liquid hit my belly, it spread like ripples in a lake. My stomach unclenched and released. A tension I didn't even realize I held in my shoulders vanished and most of the fear I had instinctively felt was replaced by a gentle calm.

The woman across from me also sipped her brew. "Iliana," she began. She stared at the table, her eyes refusing to meet mine again. "I knew we would have to meet someday. I'm sorry I had to wait for so long and I'm sorry your friend had to get hurt."

Noah. A pain pierced my heart. "What happened to Noah? What do you have to do with that?"

I felt emotions boiling and bubbling inside me and without thinking, I sipped the tea and they were instantly calmed.

"To explain that you are going to need to listen to some very difficult-to-believe facts. I am going to need you to actually listen to what I say, no matter how absurd it may seem."

I looked to Momma and she nodded. I looked back at the woman. Our eyes locked and I silently agreed.

"My name is Aphrodite," she started.

A sound, a scoff, maybe, escaped me. I looked to Momma again but this time with disbelief. She nodded once more and I looked back to the woman.

She, who claimed to be the goddess of love and beauty, continued. "Don't think of me as I am known from the old legends. Like most religions, much of that was embellished to make a better story or are outright lies. I have many powers, far beyond making tea," she smiled at her attempt to lighten the mood. When I did not return the smile, she cleared her throat and continued her story. "The skill I am most known for is my ability to control emotions."

I looked down at my tea.

"I don't need potions to do it," she said. "I gained a bit of a reputation and people would come to me to ease their sadness but mostly to bring love into marriages that were made for reasons of anything but. So, I earned my title as goddess of love and I thought I was making people happy." Her eyes suddenly turned sad. "But then I fell in love for myself." She made a little choking sound. "I thought Adonis was everything I needed." Her jaw shook a little and her eyes became more liquid. She took a sip of tea to steady herself. "But then he was taken from me. And I felt pain, true pain, for the first time in my life. I wanted to die and I walked out into the ocean alone. But I am born of water so I cannot drown. I drifted for days in my misery. Then it occurred to me that half of those people I thought I had helped would feel this pain. One lover would always die first. I realized I didn't wish this on anyone and swore to never use my powers to create love again. My son, Erose, took up the mantle but he is far more frivolous." She sighed. "One hundred and thirty-seven years later, I saw Adonis again at a market in Spain. I approached him and he knew me but could not remember me. I believe you mortals would call us soul mates if I had a soul. Shortly after our passionate reunion, he was killed again and I grieved as I bore his child and left it in the care of the Paphians who worshipped me.

"You see, the thing about souls is that they do not stay in the afterlife forever. They are sent to be reborn on Earth again. The better your soul, the shorter your wait to return. Those who are evil must stay in torment. Every hundred or so years, Adonis returns to Earth and we somehow always find each other. I never seek him out because I don't want the pain of his loss but we still find each other. I cannot resist him, despite knowing our fate. We reunite and my heart is always broken. It is my curse for interfering with the lives of mortals. It has been going on for millennia after millennia and it never gets easier. Many times, it results in a child that I have to give to my disciples." She looked at Momma. "Your momma is one of the last followers of the old ways and probably my only true friend."

Momma put her hand on top of the goddess's and smiled.

"So, I am the daughter of the Goddess of Love and her reincarnated boyfriend?" I screwed up my face in disbelief. "What exactly is in your tea?"

"It's the truth," Momma assured me.

"Think about it, Iliana. You have always absorbed the emotions of those around you," Aphrodite said.

"Momma always said I was an empath," I retorted.

"Empaths *feel* others' emotions. You *feed* on them. Ever since you reached biological maturity, men are drawn to you like gravity."

"Not Noah," I said softly with a surprising note of defiance.

"No, not Noah. His affection for you was genuine from the start. Your powers didn't work on him because they didn't have to."

"Then what happened to him?"

She traced the rim of her mug delicately with one fingertip. "You were starving."

"What do you mean?"

"You draw on the life force of others whether you mean to or not. You have kept yourself hidden, shut off from others, and starved yourself. Today, when your and Noah's emotions were highest and you kissed, you had a taste. And just like anyone who is starving, you had to have more. You lost control and sapped him of his life force."

"You do realize how crazy all of this sounds, don't you?" I asked with typical teenager condescension.

"What did I tell you at the very beginning of this conversation?"

I mulled on that for a minute. "So, what am I supposed to do?"

Aphrodite stood slowly. As she did, her skin began to let off a soft, yellow glow. It was not like she was on fire, but she herself was the source of light. She slid her foot out of her braided sandal and touched it gently to the kitchen floor. In that precise spot grew a bush of perfect, beautiful red roses.

She crossed over to me and lifted my gaze gently with her hand under my chin. "Each day you must boil a petal from one of these roses and drink the tea. It will suppress your powers of attraction so men will not flock to you. But you must not starve yourself again. You must take small amounts of energy from many people."

"And what if they end up like Noah?"

"You must have self-control. Little amounts. Many people. Noah will live but if you lose yourself again, the next person may not be so lucky."

"I'm a monster," I whispered.

"You are a succubus, Honey. Just like all of my half-mortal daughters. You are not a monster, you just have complicated powers."

"Why have you stayed away?" I hadn't expected the question to erupt from me like it did.

Aphrodite seemed to be expecting the question, however. "Because I had to." Her eyes became liquid again. "It is forbidden for us to raise or even interfere with the lives of half-mortal children unless they become dangerous to themselves or others. Most don't even know what they are or that they are even using powers to climb political ranks, to become healers, predict the stock market, etc. If I break that rule, I cannot be killed, so I face punishment worse than death." She stepped in front of me and gently touched my cheek. "I'm sorry it has to be this way. I truly am."

"Iliana! Get up or you're going to be late for school!" Momma's voice careened up the stairs and through my bedroom door.

I opened my eyes and tried to make sense of my surroundings. I was warm in my bed wearing my favorite pajamas. Outside my window, there was a gentle, golden glow on the horizon. My bookbag rested beside my door, waiting to be carried to class. I wiggled my toes under my sheet and felt the soft cotton against my skin. I rolled onto my back and touched my face. I felt like me. I giggled to myself. Aphrodite's daughter. What a ridiculous dream

"Iliana!"

I pried myself from the warmth and comfort of my bed, dressed in my standard uniform of a baggy, black hoody and jeans, and pulled my hair into a ponytail on top of my head. I grabbed my bookbag and bounced down the stairs. I was still musing over my silly dream when I rounded the corner and saw it. I stopped and my breath caught in my chest. My eyes refused to blink. There stood the rosebush, sprouting from the floor beside the table.

Momma set a steaming mug of water on the table. She looked from me to the bush and back to me.

"Yes, dear," she said. "It's all true."

I shook my head. "No. No, it can't be."

"But you know it is. Everything that has happened, everything that you have ever caused ever since you were a little girl finally makes sense."

I held my lower lip in my teeth and felt my eyes sting from tears. I didn't want it to be true, but she was right. But if last night was real, that meant Noah... I felt my chest become hollow and my cheeks were suddenly wet.

Momma pulled me into a tight hug. "It's okay. Nothing's really different now. You just have more information than you did before." She held me away from her and kissed my forehead. "Come. You must drink your rose petal before school."

I positioned myself in front of the rosebush. I studied each of the cardinal-colored blooms carefully. They were each flawless in every way, not like Momma's bug-eaten bushes in the front flower bed.

"Does it matter which one I choose?" I asked.

"I don't believe so."

I selected a velvety petal from the flower closest to me and dropped it into the mug of water. The petal melted, thickening the water, and turning it the color and consistency of blood. I wrinkled my nose as I held the mug in front of my face. I suddenly decided I would rather drink liquefied pig intestines than what was in that mug.

"Drink," Momma said.

I closed my eyes, held my breath, and sipped. Where I had been expecting a heavy metallic taste of blood, there was only the sweet taste of fresh honey. I opened my eyes. It still looked like blood. I sipped again. Honey.

"How do you feel?" Momma asked. There was a hint of tension in her voice.

I thought for a moment. There were no tingly or warm sensations. I didn't feel nauseous and everything looked the same. "No different," I decided.

She nodded. "Drink it all."

I sipped again. "Momma?"

"Hmm?" She had busied herself wiping down the already clean counter with a tea towel.

"Why didn't you tell me?"

She stopped. "It wasn't my place," she said in an almost inaudible tone. "She swore me to secrecy with the promise that she would return when you needed her." She turned to face me and began wiping her hand with the same towel.

I sipped again. "Does she live on Mt. Olympus?"

A little laugh escaped Momma and she smiled. "No. The Gods live among us. They always have. That's why so many faiths have known the same gods. They just call them by different names. I believe she is currently living in the Canary Islands."

"Tropical paradise sounds good." I took another sip of my hot drink and glanced out the window, knowing there was still a kiss of frost on the ground.

"She likes to stay near the ocean. She was made from water."

"How did she know what happened yesterday? To Noah?"

"Just because she can't interact with you, that doesn't mean she isn't watching."

I sipped more of my tea. "But-."

"No more questions for now. You need to get to school. She did make me promise to give you this." She handed me a small, flat box the color of a calm lagoon.

I set my mug down and accepted the box. I opened it eagerly. The ivory-colored hinges looked as if they would shatter if I was too rough. Inside, strung on a simple gold chain, was a single, modest white seashell. As if maneuvered by unseen hands, it gently floated out of the box. The chain unclasped itself and then reconnected behind my neck. I touched the shell and every inch of my body felt enveloped in affection, like an embrace without touch.

Momma stood, tears in her eyes, but the unmistakable look of pride on her face. The moment was disrupted by the sound of the garbage truck on the street outside.

"Good, gravy! You're going to be late!"

I downed the rest of my tea before Momma shoved a cold PopTart in my hand and shoved me out the door.

The walk to school was a crisp fifteen minutes. There was just enough chill in the air to require me to keep my hood up, but not so cold that I couldn't eat my breakfast. With each step, I worried more about Noah. She said he would live, but how long would it take for him to recover? Would he be the same? Would they ask me more questions? Would I have to lie? No. We kissed and he had a seizure. That was what happened. No one needed to know more than that. After school, I would make Momma drive me to the hospital so I could see him and apologize.

I'm sorry, Noah. I'm a succubus and you were delicious. I shook my head.

As I entered the school with the mass of students released from the buses, I expected a barrage of questions about Noah, but no one asked. As a matter of fact, none of the boys tried to walk close to me or smell my hair. None of the male teachers waved at me or smiled the creepy doe-eyed grins I'd become accustomed to. I was completely and blissfully ignored. The rose tea. I smiled. I could get used to this.

As was our custom, I met Elisa in front of the trophy cases. Her eyes were puffy and her nose was red. Her bright, ginger hair, normally neatly done up in a French braid, hung around her face like a curtain.

"What happened?" I grabbed her arm.

"Ashleigh, Kirstin, and Nikki. That's what happened."

"What did they do this time?"

"What they always do. Make fun of my weight. I can usually let it roll off my back but today..." Her eyes flooded. "I'm already stressed out from exams and my mom being a mom and I just can't take it today."

A surge of anger washed over me like a tidal wave. I watched my best friend's jaw quake and she fought back tears. Elisa may have had a few extra pounds but she was healthy and a far cry from what anyone would consider fat. Well, anyone except the three most terrible freshman girls this school had ever seen. The irony of Ashleigh calling anyone fat could not possibly have been lost on her. She had a muffin top that would make the Pillsbury doughboy drool. But with that weight came cleavage that she had no shame in flaunting. That was what gave her powers of attraction not unlike my own. Coupled with a sense of superiority and an entourage just as vicious as she was and Ashleigh was the ultimate bully.

"Come on, let's go put some cold water on your face." I steered my friend through the crowd and to the restroom.

I opened the door for her but she froze before entering. Ashleigh, Nikki, and Kirstin stood in a row with their makeup bags open on the sinks. They had locked eyes with Elisa in the reflection of the mirror and she had become a gazelle paralyzed by three lionesses. Before I could say anything, she turned and fled. They laughed maliciously and returned to painting their faces.

I felt white hot with rage. I hated those girls. They had bullied Elisa since we were five. They needed to pay for years of pain they had caused.

"What are you staring at?" Ashleigh squinted her eyes at me.

I suddenly became aware that I was, in fact, not invisible. I was also aware that I feared confrontation and found myself ducking into the nearest toilet stall.

"Freak," I heard Nikki hiss.

Through the gap in the door, I could clearly see all three of them. They were laughing about boys and ignoring that I was there. I wanted revenge for my friend but what could someone like me do to the likes of them? I felt the gentle tap of the seashell against my chest. I caressed it with my fingertips and looked back through the gap in the door.

I am a succubus.

Aphrodite did say I needed to learn to control my feeding. What better livestock to practice on? I wrinkled my nose. *As long as I don't have to kiss them.* Then, without the slightest inclination or direction, I held my hands out, palms up, and fingertips in their direction. I closed my eyes and concentrated. I concentrated on their giggles and their voices. I concentrated on the emotions contained in their voices and ever so slowly, their emotions moved into me.

Ashleigh was full of joy. It was thick and oily. It was like sucking muck through a straw, but it was most definitely joy. She had just managed to turn it into something ugly.

Nikki, though laughing, tasted of disdain. It was not unlike the taste of burnt popcorn. She hated it all. She hated these girls she called her friends. She hated her family and this school. There were underlying notes of happiness that she was accepted, but she hated herself for it.

Kirstin, also laughing, radiated fear. It flowed from her like water from a tap. She feared these friends. She feared Ashleigh would turn on her one day. She feared being cast from the group and ostracized.

I hungrily lapped up these emotions.

"I'm really tired," Nikki said through a yawn.

I continued to feed.

More yawning. "Me too," I heard Kirstin say.

I continued to feed.

"I think I need to sit down." I heard Ashleigh slide to the floor.

Just a little more. I do not want to kill them. Well... I do... but I won't.

A moment later I came out of the stall. The three girls were on the floor in a heap. Ashleigh was softly snoring and Nikki had a little drool from the corner of her mouth. I giggled. Maybe I had taken a little too much. *Oops.* At the sound of the five-minute warning bell, I hoisted my backpack over my shoulder and nearly skipped to class.

I took my seat in the row next to Elisa. Her book was open on her desk and she looked at it but her eyes were unfocused. Sadness radiated from her like cold over ice.

I set my notebook and pens on my desk and looked over at her. She was not blinking. I wanted to help her. What had Aphrodite said about making people feel emotions, not just love? Maybe I could too.

I reached over and put my hand on her shoulder. I drew on the happiness I had at seeing those terrible girls asleep on the bathroom floor and the elation I had at my first (mostly) controlled feeding. I took those positive emotions and pushed them out from my heart, down my arm, through my fingers, and into her. I watched her features, wilted by sadness, return to life. Brightness returned to her eyes and color back to her cheeks. She even sat up straighter. She turned to me and smiled and I withdrew my hand.

Real happiness came when fifteen minutes into class, Ashleigh stumbled in, her hair and makeup mussed from her nap. I had to bite my fist to keep from laughing too loud.

Two periods later, I was suddenly hit with an overwhelming feeling of sadness as I walked toward my locker. Only two more classes until physics. My lab partner, my friend, was still in a hospital bed and it was entirely my fault. Guilt washed over me. It covered me. Stuck to me. Coated me like slug slime.

Just before my fingers touched the dial on the lock, I heard, "Are you ready for Friday? I think we should get it painted this week."

Noah stood next to me. His eyes were bright and animated. His cheeks were full and flush. He looked as if nothing had ever happened to him.

"Holy shit! You're here!" I blurted out.

He cocked his head and raised one eyebrow. "Where should I be?"

"When did you get out of the hospital?"

"Hospital? Did you hit your head or something?"

We stared at each other blankly for several seconds while we each tried to process what the other was saying. He had been to the hospital. The rosebush sprouting out of my kitchen floor had been proof enough that it was not just a dream. The bell rang and I nearly jumped out of my shoes.

"You going to be okay?" he asked.

"Yeah," I said through a knot in my throat. "Yeah," I said more clearly. "I must have had a weird dream or something."

"Dreaming about me? I'm not sure if I should be flattered."

I rolled my eyes.

"I'll see you in physics. I've got to go fail an AP biology exam." With that, he turned and headed down the hall.

I watched confused before I opened my locker. A single red rose fell to the floor. I picked it up. I did not know how, but I knew what it meant. She had erased what I had done to him.

"Thank you," I whispered.

Sitting next to him in class was hard. He was happy, beaming so brightly that I could feel it emanating from him. He felt mouthwatering and it took a surprising amount of will to keep myself from reaching out my hand and taking a little nibble of his aura. It was like having stuck your fingers in the frosting of a cake as you passed by but then using all of your strength to fight going back for a full bite. A bite will lead to a slice which will lead to a gluttonous indulgence and I could not risk sending him to the hospital again.

After school, we met at his house to paint the car. Whatever Aphrodite had done to Noah, she had done to his parents as well. They welcomed me in and asked if I would be staying for supper. His dad dragged up some old cans of paint and told us to help ourselves. Not able to agree on what colors to paint it, we split it down the middle. He painted the left side green with scales like a dragon. I painted my side with red flowers and a white seashell. He chided me for making my side 'girly' but I didn't care.

I thanked his parents for inviting me to share their broccoli and green pea pizza but insisted I needed to go home to help Momma. Honestly, I don't know anyone who would have stayed to eat that.

At home, Momma and I had chicken noodle casserole. It was normally one of my favorite dinners (mostly because it was one of the only edible things she could cook) but that night was different. It was not satisfying like it normally was and I knew why. I had a new kind of hunger, not just a physical one. With my belly full and the dishes washed, I retreated to my room to do some research. The internet was a vast pool of conflicting information. I wanted to know more about who and what I am. But there were traditional legends of the gods, interpretations by poets such as Homer, and several millennia of opinions and stories to sort through. Nothing positive came from researching succubae either. I tried to call out to her to ask her in person but she did not come. Aphrodite, goddess of beauty, love, and prostitutes. My mother.

Ashleigh, Nikki, and Kirstin became my test subjects and, to some extent, my cattle. I practiced drawing their energy and stopping myself when they would start to yawn. Sometimes, I would take some of it and bestow a little happiness on my classmates, most frequently the targets they bullied.

Noah and I won the car competition. He became a good friend but nothing more. He did not remember our kiss and showed no other romantic interest in me. I assumed the goddess had something to do with that and it was probably for the best for the sake of his safety.

I drank my tea every morning. Without the unwanted attention from men, I began to change. I felt free to wear shorts and t-shirts for the first time since I was around ten years old. Elisa and I could go shopping and to the movies and do teenage girl things without men trying to put their hands on my back and shoulders or following us between the stores. But, without any sense of attraction, boys whose attention I did want showed no interest either. Momma tried to remind me that genuine interest in me would get past the powers like Noah's had, but I didn't care. Elisa had started dating and I felt alone and left behind.

At seventeen, I rebelled and stopped drinking the rose petal tea. I suddenly had the attention of every human male in a one-hundred-mile radius. I was a beacon, a silent siren calling men to their doom. I lost my virginity and while I stopped myself before killing him, he lost consciousness. I cried for days over what I could have done and immediately started my tea regimen again.

With college quickly approaching, I had to decide where to go because I couldn't take the rosebush with me. I had tried plucking a few extra pedals and taking them to school one day to see what would happen, but by afternoon they had dried and desiccated. I would have to pluck the petal fresh every morning. The bush was a shackle, chaining me to home where Momma could keep an eye on me or risk what might happen without it.

So, I stayed home and chose a school forty minutes away. It wasn't what I wanted, but it was the safest way. I dated a little as I met men who really liked me despite my powers and the tea that was meant to subdue them. They were all wonderful men who I felt for deeply but I could never achieve true intimacy with them for fear of what I might do. Without that key relationship ingredient, they would lose interest, sometimes we would fight, and the relationship would end.

When we were twenty and in our second year of college, Elisa called me from her school in Oregon to tell me about the date she had been on with a guy named Glenn Deaton. I listened to her describe his blonde hair and blue eyes and how, despite having such a 'vanilla name' he had a "funfetti look at life." Leave it to a culinary arts major to come up with such a description. This went on every weekend and at Christmas, she brought him home. He seemed to be everything he claimed to be. Watching them together, holding hands and kissing under the mistletoe, it was obvious that there was something special. I could see it in his eyes when he looked at her when they were apart. While I was excited for her, I felt loneliness wrap around me like a familiar blanket. It swaddled me and held me tight. It became restricting and I felt it getting harder to breathe. I slipped out the kitchen door quietly and into the cold December air. I tried to take a few deep breaths and loosen my chest but instead, there was only burning behind my eyes. I was what I was and it felt like a life sentence. Solitary confinement that was not entirely self-imposed. I stood there, the cold biting through my sweater, and unable to feel my nose until I felt composed enough to rejoin the festivities.

Two years later, I was sent a video link. Glenn was on one knee and Elisa was trying not to scream. I wasn't surprised though I was a little jealous. And, of course, I agreed to be her maid of honor. Two weeks later we had an impromptu engagement party. It turned out Glenn was from a city only two hours away and still had a lot of family there who happily drove down for the occasion. Between their two families, the restaurant was packed. We had selected one of those restaurant/bar/game centers so the family members with kids could attend. Without worrying about childcare. I had just beaten Elisa's cousin at air hockey for the third round when he finally admitted he was beaten for good and I returned to the bar for another rum and coke.

As I waited for my drink, a man with an open bottle of Budweiser approached me. He had a round jaw and a neatly trimmed beard. He wore a too-tight black t-shirt to ensure every muscle possible was highlighted.

"Name's Josh," he introduced himself.

Inwardly, I rolled my eyes knowing his attention had nothing do to with my powers or his genuine interest and everything to do with his drunken desire to take home just about anything with the right body parts. Outwardly, however, I smiled politely. "Brenda," I lied.

I took the drink handed to me by the bartender and turned to walk away but Josh blocked my escape. "See that truck?" He gestured to the window. "That's mine. You like a ride in it?"

Knowing better but doing it anyway, I looked out the window. It was exactly what I expected to see. A white pickup with a paint job so pristine, it had obviously never been used to haul anything more than a keg of beer. It was enhanced with a lift kit, stacks, and American flag vinyl across the tailgate. It was the standard vehicle choice for any man who needed to feel more masculine than he was.

"So, you make poor financial decisions. Wouldn't have been cheaper to tattoo 'micropenis' across your forehead?"

"Fuck you, you uppity bitch!"

His hand came back (not the one holding the beer) as my hand warmed and I prepared to unleash a wave of depression over this man that would leave him just the right side of suicidal for weeks. But, before either of us could attack, Josh was sitting on the floor rubbing his jaw.

"That's enough!" the bartender yelled. "Guys, get your friend out of here." He gestured to two other men who could have been Josh's clones.

With a round of 'come on man,' 'she ain't worth it,' and 'that bitch will get hers,' they coaxed him toward the front door.

"You alright?" It was a calm voice I had never heard before.

I turned to see a tall man with a square jaw and sandy-colored curls. His soft, grey eyes were crinkled behind his smile and I noticed he was rubbing his left hand.

"I'm fine," I said curtly. "I can take care of myself."

"No doubt." He agreed. "I heard what you said to him. But how often does a nerd like me get to try to play hero to a pretty woman?"

I rolled my eyes (outwardly this time). "Really? How are you any different from him?"

"Well, I'm a licensed pharmacist. I doubt he's picked up a book since the fourth grade. I drive a ninety-eight Camry for the gas mileage and I don't have any facial hair."

I stared at him. He was smiling and projecting a happy, jovial demeanor but I felt anxiety radiating from him like a sunbeam.

"Look, I just really have a thing about when men put their hands on women," he finally said, anxiety gone and replaced with candor. "My mom's second husband was kind of a problem."

I nodded. "That's the first sincere thing you've said to me."

He exhaled. "Let me try this again. Hi. I'm Emery. Emery Deaton."

"Deaton? You're related to Glenn?"

"Irish twins. I'm eleven months older."

"I didn't know Glenn had any siblings."

"There's five of us total. He's the baby. He graduated high school and ran. Always kept in touch, though. And you're Brenda?"

I laughed and shook my head. "Iliana Lambros." I held out my hand.

He shook it. "Iliana. Elisa's not-sister sister."

"That's me."

"I don't think I've had a single conversation with her in which I didn't hear your name." He grinned.

"She does talk a lot."

We both laughed.

"Iliana!" Elisa ran up to me. "Jordan just challenged us to two-on-two video bowling!" She began tugging my arm.

"He's ten," I argued.

"Perfect age to learn not to run his mouth. Come on!"

"Guess I'll see you around." I waved, attempting not to spill the rest of my drink as I was led away.

"Yeah. See you around." I heard Emery call behind me.

The next time we saw each other was a year later when we walked down the aisle at Elisa and Glenn's rehearsal. The wedding coordinator had bustled us into pairs. She had fussed over exactly how my hand should rest in the crook of his arm. I felt a little wave of something run through me that caused the little hairs on my arms to stand at attention. I admit, he was quite attractive in his suit jacket.

As we waited in position at the front of the procession as maid of honor and best man, he leaned down to talk to me out of the corner of his mouth. "Glenn has been a nervous wreck. I had to put tequila in his tea last night to calm him down before he paced a hole in the floor."

I giggled. "Elisa's about the same. I used Benadryl."

"Nice choice!"

The coordinator called us to attention and we proceeded down the aisle (which was a flight of stairs). Over and over and over again. She altered little details and corrected our posture. She finally decided it was 'acceptable' when the flower girl became fussy and her orders were being drowned out by rumbling stomachs. We were dismissed for dinner. Elisa's parents, despite being divorced, had come together to make her dream wedding. They had reserved a private event room at a nearby hotel where we all sat and enjoyed salad, pasta, and wine. I sat between Elisa's half-brother and a friend of Glenn's. Throughout the meal, I could feel excitement and happiness and anxiety pulsing from the people around me. I could also feel eyes analyzing my every movement and would watch Emery quickly averting his gaze.

The next morning, I rolled out of bed, downed my rose tea like a finger of scotch, and stumbled, still in my pajamas, across the street to Elisa's mom's house. The bridesmaids, mother of the bride, father of the bride, flower girl, and a few family members all gathered before the sun rose. She had insisted that we all be together to do our hair and makeup. Her cousins, who owned a salon, had their employees come to doll us up for the occasion as a wedding gift to her. There was an electricity in the air around all the women. The men had been banished to the basement to prepare but the rest of them would not be arriving until closer to brunch as they had less paint to put on their face and spray to put in their hair. Everyone was smiling and happy though many of us were grossly under-caffeinated.

When everyone had arrived, we all began discussing what we wanted to look like. But, I seemed to be the only one who noticed that the VIP was missing. I quietly backed down the hall and up the stairs and found her in her bathrobe sitting on her old childhood bed. The anxiety coming off of her hit me in the face like a shovel.

"Tell me what's going on," I said as I knelt beside her.

She wasn't crying and her face wasn't red but she was visibly shaking. "You always could read me like a book" She half-heartedly smiled.

"Why are you scared?" I asked.

"What if I'm making a huge mistake? What if we fall out of love in a few years and end up divorced like my parents?"

I put my hand on hers. "There are a million what-ifs in this world. That's not the question you need to be asking yourself. The question you need to ask is if you woke up tomorrow and he wasn't there would you feel the same as you do today?"

She shrugged. "No. I would miss him."

"Do you see yourself ever getting to a point where you can wake up in bed without him?"

She shook her head no. "But that could change."

"It could," I acknowledged. "And we could get hit by an asteroid and all die tomorrow. But if you die tomorrow, will you die happier if you married him or if you didn't?"

She nodded slowly. "I see what you're saying but—"

"No buts!" I cut her off. "I have seen the way that man looks at you. And I have felt your energy change when you talk about him. There is absolutely no question that you two belong together."

I pushed a sense of calm through my hand and into hers. Her shoulders visibly relaxed. Her brow unfurled. Her eyes softened and she stopped shaking.

"Okay," she said with weak confidence. "Let's have a wedding."

We joined the rest of the women in the kitchen. Over the course of several hours, there were mimosas and fuzzy navels passed around in mass. I began to question whether or not any of us would actually be able to walk a straight line down the aisle. The flower girl roused around nine and the men came marching in around ten. We all stood defensively in front of the bride to keep them from seeing her and reporting back to Glenn.

Elise's wedding was held at the local winery. Outdoor tables were set with white linen and pale purple flowers. She had one head table for us all to sit at and all of the guests stood inside for the ceremony. She did not want a long ceremony. She wanted a long party to celebrate. That's all she had wanted for as long as I had known her; her tastes were elegant but simple. The bridal party was to descend the stairs from the second floor. As we stood just out of view behind a white, sheer curtain, Emery flashed me a million-dollar smile.

"You look quite lovely in that color," he said.

I felt my face get warm. He was rather attractive in his gray suit with a Periwinkle tie that matched my dress. His grown-up attire was at odds with his boyish, sandy curls but the overall effect was heart-melting.

"You clean up pretty well, yourself," I said.

The string quartet changed their tune and signaled our cue. He walked carefully with me down the stairs (my legs being somewhat shorter than his were). I looked at the podium and Glenn was just as terrified as Elisa had been. I was very proud of him for not running for it. I released Emery's arm when we reached the podium and took my place to the left. Beneath my bouquet of flowers, I turned my palm towards the groom and pushed a wave of calm over him. He continued to smile broadly and was subtly ringing his hands but he emanated much less stress than as if he was being fed to lions. We all watched as

Elisa made her appearance at the top of the stairs. Glenn began to bounce on the balls of his feet with excitement and I saw his eyes become moist. He tried not to cry when he finally got to see his wife. It was the reaction that every woman hopes for on her wedding day.

Elisa was a vision of beauty in floor-length white lace that just hugged her curves. Her cousin's employee had downplayed her freckles without completely painting over them and styled her long red hair in a French twist with ringlets framing her face. I've never seen her so terrified, excited, and happy all at once. Their energies had matched and I knew they were meant to be.

After the ceremony there was dinner and dancing. I admit I may have had a little too much champagne but it was my best friend's wedding, after all. I danced with Emery several times. I couldn't help but notice how amazing he smelled and wondered if he really smelled that good or if it was the champagne talking. I felt electrified when he put his hands on my waist to dance and felt a little craving for it if we separated for a while. By the end of the night, we had exchanged phone numbers. Elisa, of course, was over the moon and could not stop talking about how I could one day be her sister-in-law. I tried to remind her that a few dances at a wedding did not mean that we should be preparing a wedding of our own. When that didn't work, I told her I couldn't get married next anyway because I was not the one who caught the bouquet (not that I had even tried).

Two weekends later, Emery and I met at the halfway point between our two cities to go for a hike. I admit that I'm not normally stupid enough to go out into the middle of the woods with a man that I don't know but his intentions were genuine and I could feel it. I wasn't exactly a defenseless damsel in distress, either, and Glenn and Elisa assured me that he did not have a violent bone in his body. We talked about the usual things like college and work. He asked me about being adopted and if I ever felt different. He didn't (and couldn't) know the half of it. We liked the same movies and many of the same books. Then at last, as we stood on a ledge overlooking the wooded canyon, he kissed me. I melted into the kiss. I hadn't allowed myself that much weakness since Noah and I was sure to remain aware so that I would not lose control. But my God that kiss! I felt as if I were lifted off the ground.

Our romance only grew from there and having a long-distance relationship was working out quite perfectly for me. We would meet every few weeks either in my city or his or halfway in between. We would have dinner and go to shows and even the symphony. Each night ended with one of those amazing and magical kisses but I always made sure there was a reason one of us could not stay the night with the other. I thankfully had Momma as an excuse as to why he could not come home with me but finding excuses not to join him for the evening at his apartment were getting harder as time went on. I knew he wanted to lay with me and I desperately wanted to lie with him. But I could not leave my rosebush and I could not lose control.

We had been seeing each other for five months that December when I made an egregious error. I had agreed to meet him in his city for a play but a snowstorm that was predicted to hit the following day came early and I was unable to make it home safely. I think he could tell that I was scared and he kept reassuring me that I had nothing to be worried about. I wished I could explain to him that HE was not what I was afraid of; I feared MYSELF. At his apartment, he set out a blanket and pillow on the couch and told me I did not have to do anything that I was not ready for. I have no words for how much I appreciated that man's patience.

He brought out a plate of cheese and dried meats and opened a bottle of wine. We played a hand of gin rummy and when the bottle ran out, we started again. I should not have had so much wine, but sitting in his apartment eating snacks and playing a simple game could not have been more perfect.

Alcohol did what alcohol does and my judgment was buried with my car in the snow outside. I'm not sure how it started but I'm fairly sure I'm the one who initiated it. His hands were warm against my skin. His lips were soft against mine. We had both wanted this for so long. We moved into the bedroom, our bodies locked together. I could feel his energy. His passion was delicious. I felt so absolutely alive.

In the morning, I woke with nausea and a little bit of a headache. It had been a while since I had had a hangover. I looked at his form in the bed next to me. He was lying on his back and his eyes were closed in a deep sleep. I put my hand on him and he was cold. I touched his face and saw the blue of his lips. No... No. No. No. No. No. No. I shook him. I tried to push the energy I had taken from him back into his lifeless body. I wept and my tears fell against his bare skin. But nothing would wake him.

"Help me!" I called out. "Please help me!"

I tried again to push energy into him.

"It won't work," her voice was calm and sad. "We cannot give life."

I turned and there stood Aphrodite in her white dress and seashell necklace and long chestnut hair.

"Please!" I exclaimed. "Please! I'm begging you!"

She shook her head. "There is nothing we can do. His life is drained. His cup is empty and cannot be refilled."

I shook my head. I cried and pushed my face into his chest. "But I love him," I said.

"I know you do," she said softly. "That's what makes it so much harder. We are not meant to love. It is our curse. You will find each other again but you will kill him again."

I looked back to the body beside me. I loved him. But I am a monster.

Chapter 39

Respiratory Infection

Pounding. Pounding.
　Thunder Drumming.
Hammer inside my head.
Coughing. Wheezing.
Can't stop sneezing.
Wishing that I was dead.
Shivering. Shaking.
Fever breaking.
Unable to get warm.
Scratchy. Itchy.
Throat is twitchy.
No voice from where it's torn.
Drinking. Sipping.
Teapot tipping.
Fluids I need to keep.
Drooping. Aching.
Brain is baking.
All I want is sleep.

Chapter 40

Onward

Ashes to ashes
    and dust to dust.
It's not easy
for the rest of us.
We remain
while you have gone.
Alone in grief.
The Reaper's won.
Your ghost remains
to haunt these halls.
Your memory painted
upon the walls.
Your scent is here,
your laughter too,
but not the whole
embody of you.
Hugs are gone
and kisses a dream.
You'd be here forever
it once had seemed.
Onward I trudge
without you there.
Unfair you've gone

and left me bare.

Chapter 41

A Christmas Poem

Christmas comes
    but once a year.
Thank the Lord
'cause this day is queer.
Christian crosses
and Pagan trees.
Jewish bread
and reindeer fleas.
Family fights
and the fat man sings.
None of these
are my favorite things.
Children squeal
and drunken hugs.
Is it New Year's yet?
Because Bah, Humbug!

Chapter 42

New Year 2024/ 2025

Once again,
    it's that time of year.
Family is close
and friends lend an ear.
Hopes are high
for what is to come.
It must be better
than what has been done.
We have cried
more than we have laughed.
It's been a river.
No one has a raft.
Sad to say
Despite hope, it's bleak.
The world has tilted
and the strong are weak.
But we stand.
Form a human chain.
We endure as one.
Until love wins again.

Cover art by Darkmoon Art

www.ingramcontent.com/pod-product-compliance
Lightning Source LLC
LaVergne TN
LVHW010215070526
838199LV00062B/4598